The most Valuable
Gift you will ever
give is a simple example

A Special Gift to:

_____

A Simple Thank-You For:

_____

Date:

_____

1001 THINGS YOUR MOTHER TOLD YOU

(and you should have listened to!)

1001 THINGS YOUR MOTHER TOLD YOU

(and you should have listened to!)

QUOTES, SAYINGS, AND TIMELESS WISDOM

CROFT M. PENTZ

Tyndale House Publishers, Inc.
Wheaton, Illinois

Library of Congress Cataloging-in-Publication Data

Pentz, Croft M.
    1001 things your mother told you : and you should have listened to / Croft M. Pentz.
      p. cm.
    ISBN 0-8423-4013-0 (sc)
     1. Maxims. I. Title: One thousand one things your mother told you. II. Title: One thousand and one things your mother told you. III. Title.

    PN6301 .P36 2001
    818′.5402—dc21   00-066640

Printed in the United States of America

07	06	05	04	03	02	01
7	6	5	4	3	2	1

CONTENTS

INTRODUCTION

I began to collect "zingers," or "sentence sermons," in the mid-1950s. In 1962, Zondervan Publishing House published my book *1001 Sentence Sermons,* later reprinted by Baker Book House.

For the next several decades, I continued to collect zingers. In 1990, Tyndale House Publishers published my book *The Complete Book of Zingers,* containing over 6,500 zingers. It had an unusual reception, going through ten printings in the following eight years.

Since then I have not stopped collecting zingers: from church bulletins, newspapers, and other publications; from speakers in person, on the radio, and on television. Some came from friends; some are original. It is impossible to trace every zinger's source, but to the best of my knowledge, none are copyrighted. Of course, I have no intention of using anyone's copyrighted material.

Somewhere along the line, the thought struck me that many of the zingers I had collected over the years were just the kind of thing one might expect to hear from one's mother. Like most people, I heard lots of wise sayings from my mother when I was growing up—sayings I did not remember or take to heart until later in my life. Now I am pleased to present yet another collection of zingers, *1001 Things Your Mother Told You (and you should have listened to!).*

I'm only a compiler. My desire is to spread these zingers and sayings far and wide so that many may benefit from them. Often a zinger is used only once and then forgotten. If they are placed in a book, thousands may benefit from them in their preaching or teaching, in their business, or for personal enjoyment.

Over the years I received many phone calls, letters, and personal comments from those who have used the zingers in my books. One pastor told me he used five to seven zingers every Sunday before he spoke. Businessmen tell me they use them at work.

Collecting and arranging these zingers took thousands of hours. It was sort of a hobby for me as I maintained a very heavy schedule as pastor and chaplain in a state school for the deaf. I so enjoyed putting this book together! I've used these zingers in churches, at banquets, at special gatherings, and in conversations with countless people.

Thanks to all the unknown people from whom these zingers originally came. I wish I could thank you personally. I trust the zingers will be a help, encouragement, and blessing to those who read this book, and I hope many others will be helped as you share them. Now semiretired, I plan to continue to collect zingers until the Lord takes me home.

The writer of Proverbs says, "It is wonderful to say the right thing at the right time" (15:23). May these zingers be used to help you fulfill this verse.

Croft M. Pentz

ADVERSITY

When adversity strikes us, God is ready to strengthen us.

The winds of adversity blow egotism out of us.

Adversity makes men; prosperity makes monsters.

Adversity does not make us fail—it only shows how frail we are.

Adversity is an opportunity to help others.

Adversity causes some men to break—others use it to break records.

Adversity introduces a man to himself.

Adversity is only sand on your track to prevent you from skidding.

A strong wind makes a strong tree.

No cloud can cast a dark shadow unless the sun is behind it.

Adversities do not make the man either weak or strong, but they reveal what he is.

Some things your mother told you about . . .

ADVICE

Some people always have plenty of advice and bad examples.

It is always good to be careful when you give advice, because someone might take it.

A small hint is worth a ton of advice.

Giving advice to the poor is not real charity.

Those who need advice the most usually like it the least.

Those who refuse advice cannot be helped.

No wise man needs advice and no ignoramus wants it.

The only way to attain perfection is to follow the advice you give to others.

Being told things for your own good seldom does you any.

When you speak to other people for their good, it is influence; when other people speak to you for your good, it is interference.

Adverse criticism from a wise man is more to be desired than enthusiastic approval of a fool.

Advice is like snow—the softer it falls, the deeper it goes.

Offering good advice may be great, but it's not the same as a helping hand.

You will always have thousands telling you what to do but few to show you how.

Advice is like cooking—you should try it before you feed it to others.

Advice is what we ask for when we already know the answer but wish it were different.

The trouble with good advice is that it usually interferes with our plans.

Give advice to your children when they're still young enough to believe you.

Sound advice is 99 percent sound and 1 percent advice.

Consultation is seeking others' advice when you have already decided what to do.

Telling a person to "be yourself" is the worst advice you can give some people.

Advice—like castor oil—is hard to take but easy to give.

If you listen too much to advice, you may wind up making other people's mistakes.

We all admire the wisdom of people who come to us for advice.

Often the furthest distance is between advice and help.

Half the world is always ready to tell the other half how to live.

Better to ask twice than to go wrong once.

A rebuke can be a better teacher than a compliment.

Some things your mother told you about . . .

AFFLICTION

Our afflictions are designed not to break us but to bend us toward God.

Spiritual fruitfulness often comes through the pruning knife of affliction.

Some things your mother told you about . . .

AIRLINES

When you fly, think only of three things—faith, hope, gravity.

Do the people who design airplane seats ever realize that one seat doesn't fit all?

Some things your mother told you about . . .

AMBITION

It's better to have a little ability and use it well than to have much ability and use it poorly.

Some doubt their ability but few their importance.

A great purpose leads to great achievement.

Too often we look everywhere and yearn for what we don't have.

All that you long for can be found in knowing God personally.

From birth to death many long for what they cannot reach.

The soul of man longs for something, not knowing it is Christ.

Talent is wanting something badly enough to work for it.

All progress is due to those who were not satisfied with their lot in life.

Unless there is in us that which is above us, we will be overwhelmed by that which is around us.

The one who aspires highly is the one who achieves highly.

Nothing pleases some more than being in the position of giving orders.

We should have long-range goals to keep us from being disappointed by short-range failures.

One planning to go nowhere can be sure to reach his destination.

It's useless to have a goal in life unless we have the courage and ability to help us reach it.

The danger in life is not that we aim too high but that we aim too low and reach it.

It's no crime to aim high and fail, but it's wrong to always aim low.

Always set your goals high and be sure they have God's approval.

Do not envy anybody—every person has something no other person has.

If better is possible, good is not enough.

Making an honest living should be easy since there is so little competition.

The more steam you put into your work, the louder you can whistle when the job is done.

Judging by appearances is wrong—the early bird may have been up all night.

Ambition never gets anywhere until it forms a partnership with work.

A great deal of what we see depends upon what we are looking for.

No brook is too little to seek the sea.

Many a good thing is done with wrong motives.

If you have a big head, your friends can reduce it for you—but if you have a small head, you're hopeless.

One trouble with life is that industry takes so much more effort than ambition.

It is good to wait on the Lord—as long as you keep busy while you wait.

Initiative—doing the right thing without being told.

Footprints in the sands of time are not made sitting down.

Find an idea big enough to live for and you will never be unemployed.

Ask God's blessing on your work, but don't ask him to do it for you.

It's the traveling bee that gets the honey.

Where you go *hereafter* depends on what you go *after, here.*

The House of Contentment will not be found if ambition is chosen to lead the search.

Don't learn the "tricks of the trade"—learn the trade.

You need just two things to be a success—talent and ambition.

We always intend to do more than what we get done.

We should have as much ambition at night as we do in the morning.

It is never too late to be what you might have been.

Hard work is anything you do with no goal in sight.

Anything is possible if you show up for work.

You will never stumble on anything good while sitting.

Ambition without purpose is aimless.

Some leave home to set the world on fire but return for matches.

Intelligence without ambition is like a bird without wings.

Don't spend your days stringing and tuning your instrument—start making music now!

Busy people are seldom bothered by depression.

Often those who have the ability to do great things are too lazy to do them.

A wish is a desire without any attempt to attain its end.

Altitude is determined by our attitude.

When we delight ourselves in the Lord, he will regulate our desires.

Incentive is the soul of success.

Ambition without application never broke any records.

Don't be a wanna-be for something God didn't want you to be.

To reach the top of the ladder, one must begin with the first rung.

Some things your mother told you about . . .

ANGER

Never start an argument with a person when he's tired or when he's rested.

Ulcers often come from something or somebody you hate.

Every time you give someone a piece of your mind, you add to your own vacuum.

Hate is a prolonged manner of suicide.

If you are patient in one moment of anger, you will escape a hundred days of sorrow.

If you punch a man in the nose when he calls you a fool, you may prove he was right.

Believers at war with their brothers cannot be at peace with their Father.

Those who strike the first blow confess they have run out of ideas.

Anger is only one letter from danger.

Anger is the wind that blows out the lamp of the mind.

Speak when you are angry and you'll make the best speech you will ever regret.

You cannot get things across by being cross.

Learn to be strong enough to control your anger, or it will control you.

The world needs more warm hearts and fewer hot heads.

Two can quarrel when one will not.

Hate is a luxury no one can afford.

Harboring hate toward others creates hate toward ourselves.

Mud thrown is ground lost.

If you scatter thorns, don't go barefoot.

Harshness should have no place in the Christian's life.

Anger is an acid which can do more damage to the vessel that holds it than to anything on which it is thrown.

Whatever is begun in anger usually ends in shame.

Anger and hate always defeat themselves.

Those who withhold themselves from anger are strong people.

Learn to close your mouth when becoming angry.

Anger is a gun that often kills the one using it.

An offense against your neighbor is a fence between you and God.

A hothead has never been able to set the world on fire.

An argument is a question with two sides and no end.

People who fight fire with fire usually end up in ashes.

An angry person is seldom reasonable—a reasonable person is seldom angry.

He is a fool who cannot get angry; but he is a wise man who will not.

Treat arguments like weeds—nip them in the bud.

Resentment must be uprooted if forgiveness is to flower.

Evil anger is when the justification of self is concerned.

It is easier to start a fight than to stop one.

A wise man never walks away from a fight—he runs away.

Anger—the fire you kindle for your enemy very often burns you instead.

Anger is the sand in the machinery of life.

Bitterness moves out when joy moves in.

Swallowing angry words is much better than having to eat them.

People—like pins—are useless when they lose their heads.

Unresolved anger leads to bitterness.

If you lose your head, what's the use of the rest of the body?

To get the best of an argument, stay out of it.

As long as vengeance seems sweet, there's bitterness in the heart.

Don't allow anyone to degrade you by making him hate you.

Never pick a quarrel—even when it's ripe.

Bitterness corrodes the spirit.

Hate, like a two-edged sword, cuts the one who uses it as mercilessly as it does the one against whom it is used.

The only thing improved by anger is the arch on a cat's back.

When you spill anger, it can't be mopped up.

Before giving away a piece of your mind, ask yourself: Can I afford it?

Life is too short to remember slights and insults that rob you of joy and happiness.

The best remedy for a short temper is a long walk.

Anger is never without reason, but seldom with a good one.

He who hates punishes only himself.

Hot heads and cold hearts never solved anything.

Anger opens the handcuffs to bitterness.

Suppressing resentment is like canning spoiled fruit.

Not even the fastest horses can catch a word spoken in anger.

To return evil for good is devilish; to return good for good is human; to return good for evil is godlike.

People who fly off in a rage usually end up in a crash landing.

Some things your mother told you about . . .

ANIMALS

Dogs who chase cars will end up being exhausted.

There's always free cheese in the mousetrap, but you never saw a happy mouse there.

Beware of a silent dog and still water.

Size doesn't matter much. The whale is endangered, but the ant is doing very well.

A dog has many friends because he wags his tail instead of his tongue.

Fireflies are the only creatures that are admired for getting lit every evening.

A turtle makes progress when it sticks its neck out.

The early bird may get the worm, but it's the early worm that gets caught.

Be like a woodpecker—just keep pecking away until you finish the job.

Anytime you think you have influence, try ordering someone else's dog around.

A smart mouse will have more than one hole.

He who plays with a cat should expect a scratch.

Pheasants are fools if they invite the hawk to dinner.

To love butterflies, we must learn to love caterpillars.

Some things your mother told you about . . .

ANTIQUES

What is junk to us is always an antique to someone else.

The best antiques to collect are old friends.

Comfortable chairs are worn out with hard use—uncomfortable ones survive and become antiques.

Some things your mother told you about . . .

ARGUING

Arguments that are none of your business are best stayed out of.

Every argument has two sides, except for the one you are in.

As the arguing gets hotter, truth slips unobtrusively away.

When you win an argument, you may lose the friend you were arguing with.

The best way to argue for your religion is to live by as much as you have of it.

The louder the arguer, the weaker the argument.

It is the reply that starts the argument.

Hot arguments have a way of providing cold shoulders.

Some people would rather lose an argument than remain quiet.

Conflict is inevitable—combat is optional.

If you are right, what's the use of arguing, and if you are wrong, what's the use?

Some things your mother told you about . . .
ATHEISM

A Christian cannot be an atheist, but he can live like one.

There is no good excuse for ignoring God.

Some things your mother told you about . . .
AUTHORITY

Those in authority are always tempted to use their authority for selfish purposes.

True Christians don't seek authority—but seek to serve others.

One cannot have authority without having responsibility.

Nothing is more likely to destroy one than authority.

progress onling
it's hard to back out

A SMALL HINT worth a TON of Advice

It is bad Manners to talk when your Mouth is full and your Head is EMPTY

B

Some things your mother told you about . . .

BACKSLIDING

A cross-eyed Christian keeps one eye on the Lord and the other on the world.

The moment God ceases having first place in your life, you have backslidden.

If you have left the Christian pathway, turn right.

The easiest road always heads downward.

Separation from Christian friends begins with a separation from God.

You cannot plow a straight furrow when looking back.

All growth that is not toward God is growing toward decay.

Signs of backsliding: dust on the Bible and drought in the heart.

Backsliding begins when knee-bending stops.

Being proud of overcoming sin is the first step to repeating it.

Don't run too far; you will have to return the same distance.

Christians are like ancient Rome; they are destroyed from within.

To be ashamed of the gospel is to be a shame to the gospel.

Some things your mother told you about . . .

BIBLE

God's Word is like a highway sign—you don't have to pay any attention to it if you don't care what happens to you.

One truth from the Bible is worth more than all the wisdom of man.

Not all biblical promises carry an unconditional guarantee.

We must adjust ourselves to the Bible—never the Bible to ourselves.

The Bible is meant to be bread for daily use, not cake for special occasions.

The blood of Christ makes us safe—the Word of God keeps us safe.

Base your life upon God's Word—not opinions.

One of the marks of a well-fed soul is a well-read Bible.

The Bible tells it like it is and like it should be.

The Christian who is careless in Bible reading is careless in Christian living.

If you study the Scriptures "hit or miss," you're likely to miss more than you hit.

If we examine the Word, the Word will examine us.

Let God's Word fill your mind, rule your heart, and guide your words.

Many people believe God's Word until it starts disagreeing with other things they believe.

Too many people keep their Bibles on the shelf instead of in their hearts.

The devil is not afraid of a Bible that is covered with dust.

It's easy to look back and see how God kept his Word; it's harder to look forward and trust him to keep his Word.

The opinion of man is no substitute for the Word of God.

A cake may satisfy for a time, but it won't take the place of your daily bread.

As long as we stand upon God's Word, Satan is a defeated foe.

Some people don't like the Bible because it cramps their lifestyle.

The Bible is like a telescope—to look through and not at!

To get much from the Bible, do not read anything into it, and let nothing be unread in it.

God does not open the windows of heaven to the person who keeps his Bible closed.

A man is rich according to what he is, not according to what he has.

Open your Bible prayerfully, read it carefully, obey it joyfully.

Study the written Word to know Christ, the Living Word.

The Bible fits man for life and prepares him for death.

The most dangerous of all false doctrines is the one seasoned with a little truth.

Many people treat the Bible like a drunk treats a light post—for support.

The Bible should be an everyday book for us.

The world doesn't read the Bible much, but it reads Christians.

You deprive yourself of the best there is when you fail to accept the knowledge contained in the Bible.

The Bible is more than a textbook—it's the textbook of life.

The only opposition to the Bible is a sinful life.

The world says, "Do and live"—the Bible says, "Live and do."

He who only samples the Word of God never acquires much of a taste for it.

To the wise, the Word is sufficient.

Measure your life to the level of the Bible—do not bring the Bible down to your level.

A closed Bible will mean a closed heart and mind.

Every factor of the Bible is meant to be a factor in life.

Apply thyself wholly to the Scriptures and the Scriptures wholly to thyself.

The Ten Commandments are not multiple choice.

The most important part of doctrine is the first two letters.

To shrink spiritually, simply close your Bible.

A dusty Bible leads to an impoverished life.

Don't change the Bible—let the Bible change you.

To stay on course, trust the unfailing compass of God's Word.

The Word of God tends to make larger-minded, noble-hearted men.

The Bible may be old, but its truths are always new.

Without a heart for God, we cannot hear his Word.

People who trust God's Word should be people who can be trusted.

You can learn a lot from the Bible; you can learn still more practicing it.

A Bible stored in the mind is worth a dozen stored in the bottom of one's trunk.

Your life will run smoother if you go by "The Book."

To be a healthy Christian, don't treat the Bible as snack food.

More people are troubled by what is plain in Scripture than by what is obscure.

Stop wrestling with God's Word and start resting on it.

To have stable roots, you must be rooted in God's Word.

Take in the Word to keep out the world.

Always examine all religious teaching in the light of the entire Word of God.

Some people make the Bible say what they want to hear.

God will not open the door to wisdom to the one who keeps his Bible shut.

A closed Bible will mean a closed heart.

In a changing world you can trust God's unchanging Word.

If God's Word dwells in you, the love of Christ shines through you.

When you open your Bible, ask the Author to open your heart.

If you pore over God's Word, his cleansing power will pour over you.

The word "but" is the "stop, look, listen" sign of the Bible.

How to expose error? Expose it to the light of God's truth.

The purpose of the Bible is to light our way, not to cover our tracks.

Stand upon God's Word and you won't fall into error.

To get a clear picture of Christ, study the Bible.

The Bible doesn't need to be revised—it needs to be reread.

If your Bible is in good shape, you probably aren't.

The Bible is true whether or not people accept or believe it.

If accepted, God's Word will expose, convict, and overcome evil.

The Bible's teaching is not hype—it's hope.

Ignoring the Bible invites disaster.

God's Word doesn't need defenders—just witnesses.

When the Bible becomes a part of you, you'll be less likely to come apart.

The Bible includes both a welcome and a warning.

Only when we are grounded in God's Word can we rise to new heights.

The Bible is the best TV guide.

Reading the Bible without meditating on it is like eating without chewing.

It's a heavy responsibility to own a Bible.

If we look at the Bible, we see a book. If we look through the Bible, we see God.

It's better to live one verse of God's Word than to memorize a whole chapter.

Opening your Bible can be a real eye-opener.

The Spirit of God uses the Word of God to change the people of God.

One revealed truth from the Bible is worth more than all the wisdom of men.

The best stress tablet you can take is the Word of God.

There is nothing like a cool, refreshing drink from the Word of God.

You haven't really learned God's Word until you have lived the Word.

God speaks through his Word to those who listen with their hearts.

The Bible isn't only for information but also for inspiration and transformation.

We don't really know the Bible unless we obey the Bible.

Like a compass, the Bible always points you in the right direction.

Take God's promises to heart, but never take them for granted.

The more you read the Bible, the more you love it. The more you love it, the more you will read it.

God's Word is an arrow that never misses its mark.

If your life depended on knowing the Bible, how long would you last?

Some things your mother told you about . . .
BOOKS

Be careful of the books you read and the company you keep.

A classic book is praised by many but read by few.

Many people long for eternal life but cannot amuse themselves on a rainy evening.

Choose any author as you choose a friend.

If you want a new idea, read an old book.

Some things your mother told you about . . .
BOREDOM

A bore never runs out of conversation—just listeners.

The things we don't like are always boring—what we like, regardless how tiring, are never boring.

A yawn is at least an honest opinion.

Yawning is usually the act of a person inadvertently opening his mouth when he wishes others would shut theirs.

CHANGE

The only constant thing in this life is change.

Those who never adapt to change will never learn to trust God.

All things in the world will change, but God's love never will.

It's important and necessary to change things in our lives from time to time.

Opinions are things you must change occasionally if you expect to improve them.

Change is often desirable, frequently necessary, and always inevitable.

Change can be one of the hardest forms of work.

When you're through changing, you're through.

There can be change without improvement, but no improvement without change.

The world will never improve unless we do.

Living involves tearing up one rough draft after another.

Things aren't what they used to be, but, praise the Lord, neither are we.

What is applicable, apply; what is not, modify.

To make a difference in the world, let Jesus make the difference in you.

Where we can't invent, we can at least improve.

To advance, we sometimes have to turn around.

When you can't change the direction of the wind, adjust your sails.

When there is a difference in you, you'll make a change in your world.

God doesn't make people nicer—he makes them new!

Don't wait for it to happen—make it happen!

Some things your mother told you about . . .
CHARACTER

We build better lives when we make long-range plans.

The direction we are facing has a lot to do with our destination.

True worth consists in being able—not in seeming to be.

The world often passes without recognizing the man of true worth.

True worth needs no interpreter—it is known by its deeds.

What people become in life depends on how they build their lives on the small and seemingly unimportant things.

Those who build walls instead of bridges have lonely lives.

A person can't keep others from having bad opinions of him, but he can keep them from being right.

If you build on Christ, your structure will stand secure.

Virtue has many preachers but few martyrs.

Rarely do we like the virtues we don't have.

Virtue can see its duty regardless of how great the darkness!

To have good character, be careful of your choices.

You cannot dream yourself into character—you must hammer and forge it yourself.

Our character grows or declines according to what we do.

You cannot build a perfect character by patching up a faulty one.

Keep your good character for what it is, for it will be your greatest wealth.

Only a truly big person can graciously accept a favor he doesn't deserve and may never be able to repay.

Your witness is only as strong as your character.

You teach *little* by what you *say,* but you teach *most* by what you *are.*

Good character, like good soup, is usually homemade.

No one knows the age of the human race, but everyone agrees it's old enough to know better.

There is no better test for a man's character than his behavior when he is wrong.

If you don't act your age, don't tell it.

The test of your character is what it takes to stop you.

Character is property—it is the noblest of possessions.

Character is a victory—not a gift.

Virtues are learned at a mother's knees—vices at some other joint.

Ability may get you to the top, but character will keep you there.

What you will be tomorrow, you are becoming today.

You can borrow brains; you can't borrow character.

To know a man, listen carefully when he mentions his dislikes.

Virtue is as good as a thousand shields.

If a man has to stand on his dignity, he is very short.

The sure way to gain respect is to gain it by conduct.

Morals without the Christian faith will wither and die like seed sown upon stony ground among thorns.

Character is like the foundation of a house—it's below the surface.

It's easy to have a balanced personality—just forget your troubles as easily as you forget your blessings.

A good test of character: when you do wrong, do you take the blame?

Christian character is not an inheritance—you must build it yourself.

Character is what you are in the dark.

Character is what you are when you are away from where you are known.

No amount of riches can atone for poverty of character.

Where we are and what we do advertise what we are.

True character is not in position or state of life, but in service.

If you are right on the inside, it usually shows on the outside.

People don't make you what they say you are; it's what you really are that makes you.

The best part of beauty is that which no picture can ever express.

The chief end of man is not to break records but to build character.

You can tell a man's character by what he turns up when offered a job—his nose or his sleeves.

Personality may open many doors, but it's character that will keep them open.

Our deeds determine us as much as we determine our deeds.

Our private lives are more important than our public image.

It matters not what you are thought to be but what you are.

Personality is what you are with other people—character is what you are when you are alone.

The way you teach is very important, and what you teach is even more important; but how you live is most important.

Be sure your faith and morals are as fresh as your daily food.

Nothing which is morally wrong can ever be politically right.

Better to be known as a do-gooder than a do-nothing.

A well-rounded character is square in all his doings.

There are two kinds of people: those to whom roses have thorns, and those to whom thorns have roses.

How we behave reveals what we truly believe.

Character is defined by what you are willing to do when the spotlight has been turned off, the applause has died down, and no one is around to give you credit.

Character is the best heritage any man can leave his children.

Behave in such a manner that people look up to you and not down on you.

Character is revealed after you've failed several times.

Integrity is Christlike character in working clothes.

You can be robbed of what you have but not of what you are.

One's character is shown by what he does when there is nothing to do.

A pat on the back will develop character if given hard enough, often enough, and low enough.

A person's character and his garden both reflect the amount of weeding done during the growing season.

While we inherit our temperament, we must build our character.

Character is but the stamp on our souls of the free choices for good or evil we have made in life.

Art, like morality, consists in drawing the line somewhere.

How a man plays the game shows something of his character. How he loses shows all of it.

You are more impressive when others notice your good character than when you tell them about it.

Salvation is more than a reformation of habits; it's a transformation of character.

Temperamental is mostly temper and a little mental.

Christianity is worth little if it doesn't change your character.

The greatest reward for man's work is not what he gets for it but what he becomes by it.

We do wrong when we fail to do right.

Christianity is of no value unless it changes your lifestyle.

You can do without being, but you cannot be without doing.

The measure of a person is not how tall one may be, but rather how his neighbors respect him.

Charisma without character leads to catastrophe.

A fruitful character is a happy life.

Don't fellowship with the person who does not value his character.

For virtue to grow, uproot the weeds of evil.

Behavior always reveals character.

Though not visible to the eye, motives are the best measure for character.

Character is not made in crisis—it is only revealed.

Some people's character is like a grapefruit—it comes apart in sections.

The harder you work at what you should be, the less you'll try to hide what you are.

Character is not where you stand in time of comfort, but where you stand in time of challenge.

What a man *is* is infinitely more important than what he *has.*

Pure thinking builds godly character.

How we behave reveals what we believe.

To avoid cause for regret, be today what you expect to be tomorrow.

Some things your mother told you about . . .
CHILDREN

See as a child sees—the joy, the wonder, the hope.

There are two lasting things we can give our children— roots and wings.

Give some children an inch and they'll become a ruler.

The advantage of having more than one child is that one may turn out well.

Strange, when our children were young, they were smart. When they became teenagers, they acted like they were retarded.

Often it's the little child in us that makes us big.

Every child is a bundle of potentiality.

We should consider not so much what the child is today as what he may become tomorrow.

A child who knows how to pray, work, and think is already half educated.

What we leave *in* our children should concern us more than what we leave *to* them.

As parents, we are daily training our children how to raise their children.

Children are creatures who disgrace you by showing in public the example you set for them at home.

Saying yes to a child is like blowing up a balloon; you have to know when to stop.

Jesus set a child in the middle of things—many churches put them in the basement.

The parent's life is the child's copybook.

The great man never loses his child's heart.

Chances are that you will be proud of your children if you have given them reason to be proud of you.

Children have never been very good at listening to their elders, but they have never failed to imitate them.

It's unreasonable to expect a child to listen to your advice and ignore your example.

Children are like wet cement—whatever falls on them makes an impression.

A nation moves upward or downward according to its children.

To make a man—begin with a boy.

What people want in the lives of adults must be put into the lives of the boys and girls.

Children are our future parents and local, state, and national leaders.

Be careful of your life lest a child stumble over it.

If you expect children to follow God, you must learn to follow him yourself.

In an effort to provide bread for children, don't forget that children don't live by bread alone.

It's surprising how soon a child learns how to train his parents.

Children are not things to be molded but persons to be unfolded.

A child wants to find out everything by asking questions no one can answer.

Children are like mosquitoes—the minute they stop making noise, they're into something.

A baby is a small member of the home that makes love stronger, days shorter, nights longer, the bankroll smaller, the home happier, clothes shabbier, the past forgotten, and the future worth living for.

Children of the light will not be comfortable in the dark.

You can give your child too much of everything except yourself.

Self-reliance is the greatest gift a parent can give a child.

Make your children improve by speaking well of them in their hearing to others.

Children who have it all appreciate nothing.

A child's home background may explain misbehavior, but it can never excuse it.

Raising children is a matter of timing—enjoy your kids while they're young and still on your side.

Children who always get what they want will want as long as they get.

What we put into the thought stream of our children will appear in the life stream of tomorrow.

If you can't hold your children in your arms, hold them in your heart.

Hold your children's hands every chance you get—the time will come when they won't let you.

Time spent with children is never time wasted.

For most kids, cleanliness isn't next to godliness—it's next to impossible.

The surest way to make it hard for your children is to make it soft for them.

It is not mean to wean your child.

A child is a person who can dismantle in five minutes the toy you took five hours to put together.

Today's unchurched child is tomorrow's criminal.

Children can keep a family together, especially when you can't afford a baby-sitter.

Children are not only a comfort to a man when he reaches middle age—they help bring it on.

Children learn from their parents in three ways: example, example, example.

The word "no" with children carries more impact when it is balanced with "yes."

If you let your children grow without trimming their buds, don't expect many blossoms.

Children of all ages are the same—they close their ears to advice and open their eyes to example.

A child may not inherit his parents' talent, but he will absorb their values.

We often wonder about the child of tomorrow, forgetting what they are today.

The character of your children tomorrow depends on what you put into their hearts today.

One thing kids save for a rainy day is lots of energy.

Cherish your children for what they are—not what you want them to be.

No boy expects to grow up to be as dumb as his father.

Some of the best things you can give your children are good memories.

Better than having children bear your name is to have them bear Christ's name.

Helping a child is an investment in the future.

If you wait until your children agree with you, they'll never obey.

You can't give a child everything he wants without also giving him boredom.

No child outgrows the fathering from his father or the mothering from his mother.

Learning in childhood is like engraving on a rock.

Little children are a big concern to God.

If your children look up to you, you've made a success of life's biggest job.

Some things your mother told you about . . .

CHRISTIANITY

God loves his children not because of who they are, but because of who he is.

Happy is the one who walks so close to God that he leaves no room for the devil.

Christians are like pianos—grand, square, upright, but of no earthly use unless they are in tune.

Christianity is not a way of doing certain things but certain ways of doing all things.

Christians are not sinless but should sin less.

Too many Christians mistakenly think the Christian life is a playground instead of a battleground.

Christianity is not just Christ *in* you, but Christ living his life *through* you.

A Christian is one who does not have to consult his bankbook to see how wealthy he really is.

The only way to be a model Christian is to copy the perfect pattern.

Forgiven sinners know love and show love.

God's work in us isn't over when we receive Christ—it has just begun.

The Christian who wields the sword of the Spirit yields no ground to Satan.

Your identity crisis is resolved when you identify with Christ.

A true Christian is a person who is right-side-up in an upside-down world.

What God has promised in his Word to one Christian, he promises to all.

Being a Christian does not keep us from doing senseless things!

When living near Christ it doesn't matter if people love or despise us.

If you live for Christ on earth, you will live with him in heaven.

Bless God for your afflictions; thank him for your changes; praise him for your losses.

It's easy to be pious so long as things are going well with us.

If you are not as close to God as you once were, you know who moved.

Discouragement is a tool used often by Satan to destroy you and God's work.

It's a vice to covet the earthly—it's a virtue to covet the heavenly.

Let your gladness proclaim that you serve a good Master.

If you seek self-mastery, begin by yielding yourself to the Master.

To cure a sick soul, put it on a prayer diet.

Are the things you are living for worth dying for?

Jesus never taught men how to make a living—he taught them how to live.

Consider no place, however secret, a sanctuary from sin.

When full of self, there's no place for Christ.

Of all Christian failings, one of the most common is egotism.

Never elevate yourself nor demean yourself!

Being religious is human—being righteous is divine.

A true test of Christian love—help those who cannot help you in return.

Live today as you will wish you had lived when you stand before God.

A Christian is one who makes a choice and experiences a change.

Nothing touches the heart like the Cross.

If you are a Christian in small ways, you are not a small Christian.

A changed life is the result of a changed heart.

The Christian life has no time-outs.

Live so that the good inside is visible on the outside.

Our opinions become fixed at the point where we stop thinking.

It's far better to appear untrue before the world than to be untrue to oneself.

So live that everyone who comes in touch with you will contact some good.

If you are too big for a small job, you are too small for a big job.

Take a firm hold on life just where you are.

The future belongs to him who can grow.

We will grow in the direction in which we express ourselves.

We grow through doing—unused power and unused muscles remain undeveloped.

Christianity has not been tried and found wanting—it has been tried and found difficult, so many cease trying.

Christianity is no mere religion—it is a life.

If you want to defend Christianity, practice it.

The best argument against Cristianity is an inconsistent Christian.

Good and evil will always be in conflict with each other.

All Christians must fight if they expect to win a crown.

Regardless of how fully equipped we may be, we fight at a disadvantage when we have a guilty conscience.

The way we view eternity will affect the way we live in time.

The right kind of heart is a kind heart like God's.

The Christian's walk and talk must go together.

The fruit of Christian unity grows out of our union with Christ.

As life's shadow lengthens, thoughts of God should deepen.

The armor of God is awkward apparel for sitting in armchairs.

Whether or not one is a misfit depends upon what he is supposed to fit.

Christianity is not a formula for explaining everything.

We may not walk to the martyr's stake, but we must walk in the Master's steps.

Never mind trying to remember the seven dwarves or the eight reindeer—just remember the Ten Commandments.

Christians on fire for God will attract sinners to the light.

The more Christ's love grows in us, the more his love flows from us.

A rock-solid believer thrives even in a sin-hardened place.

Don't be so busy doing good that you neglect to do what's right.

Living for God leaves a lasting legacy.

Christians are a part of a fellowship as wide as the world and as high as heaven.

Christ's disciples are called to disciple others.

Decorations stay clean; disciples get dirty.

Christian living is what you do with both your mind and hands.

Drawing close to Christ produces a growing Christlikeness.

An upright man can never be a downright failure.

We should teach people not only to walk but where to walk.

If you want to defend Christianity—live it.

If you want today's fire to burn brightly, begin by throwing out yesterday's ashes.

The Christian life doesn't get easier, it gets better.

When growth stops, decay begins.

A sure sign of spiritual growth is the ability to take criticism.

A half-hearted Christian is just half a Christian.

What we practice proves what we profess.

Christianity is no escape from difficulties.

If your Christianity doesn't work where you are, it won't work anywhere.

Some things your mother told you about . . .

CHRISTIAN LIVING

Some of the worst sins of Christians are the sins of omission.

The careful foot can walk anywhere.

When you stand straight, don't fear a crooked shadow.

The straight-and-narrow road has the lowest accident rate.

On the "straight and narrow," traffic is all one way.

He who walks with God will never be late for his spiritual meals.

The theory of relativity does not work in real life.

Loving God with all the heart will take the kinks out of the head.

One proof of our love for our Father is how much we love his children.

A lame man on the right road will beat a fast runner on the wrong road.

Intelligence enables a person to catch on—wisdom enables him to let go.

The safe and sensible course is midway between two extremes.

For every effect there is an adequate cause.

Those who live with too much tension seldom live to enjoy a pension.

Don't only commit the Golden Rule to memory—practice it in your life.

The greatest distance we have yet to cover lies within us.

People are rich according to what they are, not what they have.

Do not get ahead of God—he may not follow you.

It is better to live for Christ than to wish you had.

Christians are at their best when everything else is at its worst.

Christians show what they are by what they do with what they have.

To keep spiritually fit, keep walking with the Lord.

A broken heart is the first step to spiritual wholeness.

You cannot run the race until you learn to walk.

Wait for him—work for him—watch for him.

Some things your mother told you about . . .

CHRISTMAS

There is always the danger of keeping Christmas and losing Christ.

If you have Christmas joy in your heart, let it show on your face!

Unless you see the cross overshadowing the cradle, you will have lost the real meaning of Christ's birth.

Santa Claus causes most parents to say, "Owe, owe, owe."

Full hands cannot accept God's Christmas gift—Jesus!

Some things your mother told you about . . .

CHURCH

Whether or not a person goes to church regularly does not depend on how far he lives from church but rather on how far he lives from God.

You will enjoy the service more if you do not sit in the seat of the scornful.

Some things your mother told you about . . .

COMMITMENT

Forget that you cannot do enough; it is enough to do whatever you can.

Are you planning to do God's work or working to do God's plan?

Fellowship with Christ is the secret of fruitfulness for Christ.

A life given fully to God becomes a God-filled life.

If you want God to go with you, you must go with God.

Nothing quiets criticism like involvement.

Consecration—not perfection—is the mark of a saint.

Commitment is more than putting Christ first—it's keeping him first.

Some things your mother told you about . . .

COMPASSION

It's much easier to tell a person what to do with his problem than it is to stand with him in his pain.

A hurting person needs a helping hand—not an accusing finger.

Sympathy is a gentle nature shining through gracious deeds.

Train your heart to give sympathy and your hand to give help.

Compassion offers whatever is necessary to heal the hurt of others.

God doesn't recycle his mercies—they are new daily.

The people we like the least may need our love the most.

Some things your mother told you about . . .

COMPLAINING

Some cry so loud about their hard luck that they can't hear opportunity knocking.

The one who complains the loudest is generally the one who contributes the least.

Where complaining exists, thankfulness is absent.

Please don't pray for rain if you are going to complain about the mud.

Don't complain—every lamb that bleats loses a mouthful of hay.

It's easy to complain when things aren't going your way—those who can rejoice at these times are true Christians.

There's something wrong with both a person and a motor when they keep knocking.

One problem of being a grouch—you have to make new friends each week.

Frustration is not having anyone to blame but yourself.

Usually it is littleness of spirit rather than greatness of trouble that makes us complain.

Those who are good at complaining are seldom good for anything else.

It's easier to complain about something than to work and change it.

Complaining, like other vices, can be habit-forming.

God is so good that it would appear there should be no complainers in the world.

We dishonor God when we complain about our lot in life.

Some people speak constantly of the beauty of the roses—others speak always of their thorns.

Complaining is more than words; it's seen in our attitudes and actions.

Don't worry about the potholes in the road—enjoy your trip.

A squeaky wheel doesn't always get the grease. Sometimes it gets replaced.

Even when you have pains, you don't have to be one.

What you're complaining about today you may be reminiscing fondly about tomorrow.

Growl all day—and you'll end up dog tired.

Whines are the products of sour grapes.

Those who beef too much may find themselves in the stew.

He who kicks up a storm should expect rough sailing.

You're already cooking up trouble when you stew about tomorrow.

Those who complain about rising early are better off than those who are unable to rise.

Look around at what you have before you complain about what you don't have.

Many people are born crying, live complaining, and die disappointed.

Some things your mother told you about . . .

COMPROMISE

You begin to compromise the moment you depart from God's Word.

Compromise is putting water in the milk and selling it for pure milk.

Compromise is simply failing to live up to the best of what you can be.

Those who make small concessions are soon eaten alive.

If it seems you are going around in circles, perhaps you are cutting too many corners.

There's a vast difference between tolerance and compromise.

It's all right to compromise in policy but never in principle.

Compromise is always wrong when it means sacrificing principle.

Some things your mother told you about . . .

CONCEIT

A conceited person never gets anywhere because he thinks he is already there.

Self-conceit always grows on thin soil.

The best remedy for conceit is to sit down and make a list of all the things you don't know.

Some things your mother told you about . . .

CONSCIENCE

Conscience is the only mirror that does not flatter.

Never tamper with your conscience—it is the soul's compass.

Never break faith with conscience.

Conscience can be our compass if the Word of God is our chart.

An imperfect conscience needs a perfect guide.

Conscience is an inner voice to remind us that Someone is looking.

Conscience is a safe guide only when guided by God.

A clear conscience knows no fear.

Conscience doesn't keep you from doing certain things—it just keeps you from enjoying them.

A clear conscience, like a soft pillow, helps you sleep well.

When we lose the sense of God, we lose the sense of sin.

The testimony of a good conscience is worth more than a dozen character witnesses.

A quiet conscience brings peace and rest.

Conscience is God's presence in man.

A man's conscience tells him what he shouldn't do but does not keep him from doing it.

Deal reverently with your conscience—it is a gift from God.

There is no place to hide sin without your conscience looking in.

Are you living close enough to God where you can feel him nudging you?

The conscience is a small voice deep down inside where the acoustics are generally poor.

A scar in the conscience may disfigure your soul forever.

The best tranquilizer is a clear conscience.

Few things instill more courage than a good conscience toward God.

Man should be the master of his will and the slave of his conscience.

A guilty conscience needs no accuser.

Conscience is like an alarm clock. If you don't pay attention to it, it will soon cease to wake you up.

Every moral breakdown is the result of a dulled conscience.

A good conscience is the best friend you will ever have.

Some things your mother told you about . . .

CONTENTMENT

Most people are unhappy when they get what they deserve.

Some people are never satisfied, always wanting something.

All you have belongs to God—he has made you in charge while on earth.

The more you have, the more you are in debt to God.

To have is to owe—not own.

The greatest of all possessions is self-possession.

The more of heaven there is in our lives, the less of earth we shall covet.

All you need to know to be content is this: God is good.

It's what's in your heart that makes you thankful, not what's in your pocket.

It takes a mighty conscientious person to know where contentment ends and laziness begins.

A wise person will desire no more than he may acquire justly, use soberly, distribute cheerfully, and leave contentedly.

Fortify yourself with contentment, for this is an impregnable fortress.

Contentment is natural wealth.

Not what we have, but what we enjoy, constitutes our abundance.

Discontent is the penalty we must pay for being ungrateful for what we have.

There are two ways of being rich. One is to have all you want, the other is to be satisfied with what you've got.

Contentment isn't getting what we want but being satisfied with what we have.

It's better to appreciate things you don't have than to have things you don't appreciate.

If you cannot have everything, make the best of everything you have.

There is very little difference between doing what you like and liking what you do.

Enough is usually a little more than we possess.

If you don't enjoy what you have, how would you be happier with more?

How to find contentment? Count your blessings instead of hardships.

He who lives content with little possesses everything.

Be content with your lot; *never* be satisfied with your achievements.

Make the most of all that comes and the least of all that goes.

If you don't make a living, live on what you make.

If you don't get what you want, want what you get.

Contentment is a matter of hoping for the best and making the best of what you get.

Contentment can make poor people rich—discontentment makes rich people poor.

The secret of contentment is knowing how to enjoy what you have.

Wealth is in the head—not in the hand!

The riches that are in the heart cannot be stolen.

To be content with little is difficult; to be content with much is almost impossible.

Most of us get run down because we stay wound up.

The Lord is my shepherd; that is all I want.

He who wants little always has enough.

Those who are content are never poor—those who are discontent are never rich.

He who has little and wants less is richer than he who has much and wants more.

How you handle your problems by day determines how you sleep by night.

If you don't get what you like, try to like what you get.

For every want that is satisfied, another steps in to take its place.

We can be sure we are not pleasing God if we are not happy with ourselves.

Few are satisfied with what they have accomplished in life so far.

There are more things than we realize that we do not really need and can get along very well without.

He is truly rich who has a contented mind.

If you got everything you wanted, where would you put it?

Resentment comes from looking at others; contentment comes from looking to God.

Cheerfulness and contentment are great beautifiers and are famous preservers of youthful looks.

Contentment is not the fulfillment of what you want but the realization of what you already have.

A contented person can enjoy the scenery on a detour.

Be dissatisfied enough to want to improve, and be satisfied enough to be happy.

Discontentment is the penalty we pay for being ungrateful for what we have.

Most people would be satisfied with enough if others didn't have more.

Some things your mother told you about . . .

COOPERATION

The love that unites Christians is stronger than the differences that divide them.

Remember that though there are big apples on top of the basket, it's the small ones on the bottom holding them up.

Christians are like coals of fire—together they glow, apart they die out.

Those who are drawn toward Christ are drawn toward each other.

Learn to be an assister, not a resister.

To work effectively with others, learn to compromise intelligently.

If you can't help, don't hinder.

The world has too many cranks and not enough starters.

Never cut what can be untied.

It's the "unity" in community that gets the job done.

Teamwork divides the effort and multiplies the effect.

Some change their ways when they see the light—others when they feel the heat.

Always allow space in your togetherness.

When the head and the heart are in conflict, the body becomes the battleground.

We can go a lot farther together than we can alone.

If there's no harmony in your life, try changing your tune.

If you want to gather honey, don't kick over the beehive.

We need to stay yoked up with the one who is able to carry the load.

Christians may not see eye to eye but can walk arm in arm.

Satan divides and conquers—Christians unite and conquer.

Some things your mother told you about . . .

COURAGE

Courage is not only standing for what's right, it's doing what's right.

Courage is holding on just a few minutes longer.

Those who act faithfully will act bravely.

Anyone can praise God—it takes courage to follow him.

It sometimes takes more courage to face ridicule than to face death.

He who is fearful will never cross the sea.

A little encouragement can speak a great endeavor.

With Jesus on the inside, we can withstand any trouble on the outside.

Many a person has convictions for which he wants someone else to supply the courage.

Don't pray for the mountains of difficulties to be removed—have courage to climb them.

One man with courage is a majority.

What you once might have been, you may still have a chance of becoming.

Courage is the art of being able to say "nice little doggie" until you have time to locate a rock.

The deeper our conviction, the greater our courage to sustain it.

Correction may hold us, but courage will motivate us.

Keep your fears to yourself, but share your courage with others.

No problem is heavy if the heart is light.

Christ gives us the courage of our convictions.

Never accept a philosophy that supports a lack of courage.

Courage is the master of fear, not the absence of fear.

Courage is only built by conquering fear.

Without courage, all other virtues lose their meaning.

The courage to speak up must be matched by the wisdom to listen.

Sometimes it takes as much courage to resist as it does to go ahead.

Some things your mother told you about . . .

COURTESY

The mark of a man is how he treats a person who can be of no possible use to him.

Courtesy opens many doors.

Courtesy is understood in every language.

Nothing costs less and goes so far as courtesy.

The greater the person, the greater his courtesy.

Try this—sometimes allow the person behind you in a line to go ahead of you.

Courtesy is the oil that lubricates the frictions of life.

Some things your mother told you about . . .
CREATIVITY

Creativity often consists of merely turning up what is already there.

There is always a better way—your challenge is to find it.

Sometimes it takes a lot of scratching to get out of a situation you were just itching to get into.

The soaring eagle does not worry about how to cross the river.

It's easy to start a fire by rubbing two sticks together if one is a match.

Some things your mother told you about . . .
CRITICISM

It is usually best to be generous with praise but cautious with criticism.

Faultfinders never improve the world; they only make it seem worse than it really is.

Every time someone makes his mark in the world, someone else is waiting to use the eraser.

Don't kick a person when he is down because someday he will get up.

Any fool can criticize when a person makes a mistake—and they usually do!

Few people ever carve their way to success with cutting remarks.

Faultfinding is as dangerous as it is easy.

If you want to find fault, begin with yourself, and you'll see you need not go any further.

Even the perfect Son of God could not escape the faultfinders.

The moon is never hurt by barking dogs.

Those who can't or won't are usually the first to find fault.

To be quick to find the fault of others does not make you superior to them.

Men may misjudge your aim and think they have reason to blame, but Christ, not men, is the Judge.

Be occupied with improving yourself, and you will have little time to criticize and judge others.

Never judge a person's actions until you know his motives.

Better to err on the side of charity than to misjudge anyone.

When you criticize, are you doing it to help or to hurt?

Criticism, like charity, should begin at home.

A person who criticizes is never out of a job.

It's always easier to criticize the small mistakes of others than to look at your own mistakes.

When you point a finger at someone, you have three fingers pointing back at yourself.

Can you do the work better than those you criticize?

Do the work of those you criticize, and do it better; then others will listen and respect your criticism.

A critic is a person who is unable to do a thing the way he thinks it ought to be done.

Criticism is envy in action.

Throwing mud at a good man only soils your own hands.

Mansions in the sky aren't built out of mud thrown at others.

Whatever you dislike in another person, be sure to correct in yourself.

Nothing will be done if you wait until you can do it so well that no one will criticize.

Don't practice the habit of telling people where to get off unless you are a bus driver.

To find a fault is easy; to do better may be difficult.

It is much easier to be critical than correct.

Do not begrudge others what you cannot enjoy yourself.

Show yourself more human than critical, and your pleasure in life will increase.

Anyone can tear down a house—few are skillful enough to build it.

Never fear criticism when you're right; never ignore it when you're wrong.

If you are afraid of criticism, you will die doing nothing.

Anyone can find fault—it takes the tender and kindhearted soul to praise.

Instead of pointing a critical finger, offer a helping hand.

Many can find a fault—few find a remedy.

To belittle people, you have to be little.

How seldom we weigh our neighbors on the same scales we weigh ourselves.

Don't put people down—unless it is onto your prayer list.

It's better to be trying very hard than to be very trying.

Judge not thy friend until thou standest in his place.

Criticism from a friend is better than flattery from an enemy.

Sandwich every bit of criticism between two layers of praise.

Cynicism sees only evil at work; faith sees God at work.

We won't have time to find fault with others if we're busy seeking wisdom.

If you're not big enough to stand criticism, you're too small to be praised.

Praise loudly; blame softly.

People who have no charity for the faults of others are generally blind to their own.

To keep from looking down on others, look up to the cross.

It isn't necessary to blow out the other person's candle to let yours shine.

No donkey profits from calling another donkey "Long Ears."

All dogs in the pack yap at the leader. If you aren't being criticized, you aren't doing anything.

Don't judge those who try and fail—judge only those who fail to try.

Judge people from where they stand—not where you stand.

The fault we see in others may be the reflection of our own.

Better than fixing the blame for the breakdown is fixing the breakdown itself.

It is the person who has done nothing who is sure nothing can be done.

A small HINT is worth a TON of Advice

It is bad Manners to talk when your mouth is full and your Head is EMPTY

progress only if stick its neck out

D

Some things your mother told you about . . .

DEATH

Death is not extinguishing the light from the Christian—it is putting out the lamp because the day has come.

Fear of death is canceled by the death of Christ.

Even though we may die, God's work will continue.

Death is the last chapter of time but the first chapter of eternity.

Death accepts no bribes.

The living Savior takes the fear out of dying.

You may feel too tired and be too busy to attend church, but one day you won't be too busy or tired to die.

Faith in Christ builds a bridge across the gulf of death.

Facing death with confidence does not take away our love for life.

After death comes judgment, but before death there is hope for every person.

A person's conception of death will determine his philosophy of life.

When it's time to die, make sure that's all you have to do.

Where death finds you, there eternity will keep you.

Spiritual death removes one from the heavenly family as physical death removes one from the earthly family.

We can really live when we are ready to die.

Jesus—don't leave earth without him.

If you knew you would die tomorrow, how would you live today?

Death can take the ones we love—it cannot take our memories.

Death may take your body, but it can't take your influence.

You cannot live wrong and die right.

No one is so old that he cannot live yet another year nor so young that he cannot die today.

God's timing is perfect—even in death.

For the Christian, death is not a tragedy—it is triumph.

Death may alarm us, but it cannot harm us.

Only those who are ready to die are ready to live.

Right relationships in life ease the sting of grief in death.

There is hope beyond death, but there is hurt on this side of heaven.

Some things your mother told you about . . .

DECISION

What you hope to be like tomorrow depends on the choices you make today.

One person with a conviction is equal in force to ninety-nine who only have opinions.

Some can teach you to do and some can teach you to think, but you alone must decide what to do after thinking.

God chooses what we go through—we choose how to go through it.

If we provide for this life but take no care for eternity, we are wise for a moment but fools for eternity.

The responsibility for making wise choices should include a sensitivity to the leading of the Holy Spirit.

A person should give a lot of thought to a sudden decision.

To get nowhere, follow the crowd.

Make worthy choices, but avoid taking foolish chances.

Almost everyone knows the difference between right and wrong, but some hate to make the decision.

Some people have yet to learn that they cannot travel in the wrong direction and reach the final destination.

Your response to Christ decides if death is the doorway to gloom or glory.

Find your aim in life before you run out of ammunition.

People who jump to conclusions often land on a lie.

Don't saddle a horse that you cannot ride.

You cannot direct the wind, but you can adjust your sails.

Don't let the urgent cloud out the important.

Every man has an equal chance to become greater than he is.

Willpower is the ability to eat one salted peanut.

The person who really wants to do something finds a way; the other kind finds an excuse.

Don't agonize—organize.

The choice is simple—you can either stand up and be counted or lie down and be counted out.

Destiny is not a matter of chance; it is a matter of choice.

Some people seek to be somebody but are never specific.

Most of the troubles in life are the result of saying "yes" too soon or "no" too late.

Choices always have consequences.

God will lower the gate of warning, sound the bell, and flash the red light, but he won't keep you from crossing the tracks.

The only thing different between a rut and a groove is your frame of mind.

Opinion helps us make a decision without having information.

After we make our choices, they turn around and make us.

Better be a lame man on the right road than a good man on the wrong road.

God doesn't remove the consequences of our wrong choices.

It's not hard to make decisions when you know what your values are.

You are free to make your own choices, but you are not free to determine the consequences.

Our present choices determine our future rewards.

An opinion is something you hold—a conviction is something that holds you.

A moment of indecision can be very costly.

Indecision easily becomes a harmful habit.

Learning to make a decision after proper consideration is the most valuable habit.

The trouble with reaching a crossroads in life is the lack of signposts.

Some things your mother told you about . . .

DEDICATION

Christ deserves the same place in our hearts that he holds in the universe.

To renew your love for Christ, review his love for you.

Shape the will without breaking the spirit.

Putting Christ first brings satisfaction that lasts.

It's a sin to accept the good when the best can be had.

It behooves us to keep ourselves at our best moment by moment.

The more you love Jesus, the more you will look forward to heaven.

It's a sin to do less than your best.

It's human to stand with the crowd—it's divine to stand alone.

Some people say, "Let God go" instead of "Let go and let God."

Dedication is more than surrender—it's sharing and service.

God must first do something *for* us and *in* us before he can do something *through* us.

There is a lack of dedication when we believe in the Cross but refuse to bear our cross daily.

If you want God to be pleased with you, you must do what pleases God.

We show our love for Christ by what we do with what we have.

God will control one's possessions when he controls the person.

A Christ-centered life cannot be a self-centered life.

God gives his best to those who leave the choice with him.

May the Lord touch our hearts with his finger of love and leave a fingerprint no one can rub off.

In this world it is not what we take up but what we give up that makes us rich.

If we're not as spiritual as we *could* be, we're not as spiritual as we *should* be.

He who abandons himself to God will never be abandoned by God.

He who serves two masters will lie to one of them.

God does not look for great ability but usability.

We cannot decide whether or not we live or die; we can only decide what we will die for.

Jesus invested his life in you. Have you shown any interest?

Becoming like Christ is the one thing worth giving up everything else for.

It's not *who* you are, but *whose* you are.

God tends to use the one nearest him.

Nothing is too big for God to accomplish, and nothing is too little for him to use in accomplishing it.

Place God at the head of your priority list.

Folks who never do any more than they are paid for never get paid for any more than they do.

Walk so close to God that nothing can come between.

Few things are impossible to diligence and skill.

Christ is not valued at all unless he is valued above all.

The cure for cold feet is a heart on fire for God.

Anything that matters more to you than God is an idol.

Lasting joy comes when you put Christ first.

Following Christ has two requirements: believing him and obeying him.

Dedication is like signing your name to a contract and letting God fill it in as he wishes.

There is no great success without a great commitment.

True freedom is found in captivity to Christ.

It is better to die for something than to live for nothing.

God often uses small matches to light great torches.

God speaks when we are still enough to listen.

The nearer we come to Christ, the nearer we come together.

Every calling is great when greatly pursued.

God is seeking people who are not shopping for what they want but what he wants for them.

If God has called you, do not spend time looking over your shoulder to see who is following.

Dedication is giving your life to the one who died for you.

God always gives his better to those who give him their best.

Love God more than you fear hell.

Sacrifice in giving is a true test of love.

There will be a special place in heaven for ordinary people who did the extraordinary thing in ordinary places.

When you don't know what to do first, give the Lord first place.

When you grasp, you lose—when you yield to God, you gain.

When you give your all, your little is a lot.

Living a life of dedication does not mean living a life of isolation.

Dedication to Christ is not a one-time choice—it's a daily challenge.

Going where the Lord wants you to go will mean at one time turning your back on the crowd.

Moldable people stay in shape with God.

We can never do too much for the one who did so much for us.

Beware of a costless Christianity.

You can't turn your back on Christ if you keep your eyes upon him.

The kingdom of God cannot be built on leftovers.

You get the best out of others when you give the best of yourself.

Holding on is not always strength—sometimes letting go is.

Heavenly minded people do the most earthly good.

Dedication should come before duty.

All boats, regardless of the size, rise with the tide.

Spiritual desires will determine what we think of God.

Write your plans in pencil but give God the eraser.

You can do what you want when you want to please God.

Someone must be supreme in our lives—if not Jesus, someone else less than he.

Our Lord is not seeking compliments but commitments.

Is what you're living for worth dying for?

Anything worth doing is worth starting.

Some things your mother told you about . . .

DETERMINATION

Today's oak is yesterday's nut that held its ground.

You win some and lose some, but you have to suit up for them all.

Start each day with your armor in place and your marching orders in hand.

We can do anything we want if we stick to it long enough.

Those who say, "It can be done" never ask, "Does anyone want it done?" or "How much will it cost?"

Doing your best is more important than being the best.

A hero is no braver than an ordinary person—he's just brave five minutes longer.

Becoming number one is easier than staying number one.

You may know you can't reach the stars, but that should not keep you from trying.

One who has much push will get along without any pull.

A pound of determination is worth a ton of repentance.

The only way to make a "comeback" is to go on.

You never know what you can do until you make an effort.

If you have a hill to climb, waiting will not make it smaller.

More success is brought by determination than by talent.

Motivation may get you started, but it will take determination to keep you going.

The man who falls down gets up a lot quicker than the one who lies down.

Stand up for Christ or you'll be tripped up by Satan.

Morale is when your hands and feet keep on working when your head says it can't be done.

The triumph is not in never failing but in rising every time you fall.

Some may succeed because they're destined to, but most succeed because they're determined to.

Vision and persistence cannot be beat.

Seek to find the best in the worst, to discover the great in the small, to see beauty in the plain, and to detect the elegant in the simple.

There are possibilities in the impossible, but only for the persistent.

Determination, not desire, controls destiny.

The man who moved mountains began by carrying away small stones.

It's easier to keep up than to catch up.

Spiritual triumphs are not won sitting in easy chairs.

Not everything we face can be changed, but nothing can be changed until it's faced.

Some things your mother told you about . . .

DIET

A moment on the lips means a lifetime on the hips.

It's possible to carry a lot of weight without gaining pounds.

More people commit suicide with the fork than with any other weapon.

The best exercise in losing weight is pushing yourself away from the table.

Temperance is total abstinence from that which is evil and moderate use of that which is good.

The minutes spent at the dinner table don't make you fat—it's the seconds.

Some things your mother told you about . . .

DISCIPLINE

If you want to be a servant of others, you must be master of yourself.

Plan as if Christ's return is years away, but live as if he's coming today.

He who refuses to be controlled by others has never learned to control himself.

Discipline yourself so others won't have to.

Thinking well is wise, planning well is wiser, but doing well is wisest.

They who do not live up to their ideals soon find that they have lost them.

It is better to bite your tongue than to let it bite someone else.

Make someone happy today—mind your own business.

Fair people can disagree without being disagreeable.

Live every day as if it were your last—do every job as if you were the boss—drive as if all other cars were police cars—treat everybody else as if he were you.

God's discipline is never cruel but is always corrective.

Discipline determines the difference between success and failure.

Make the most of yourself, for that's all there is of you.

The best victory is to conquer self.

Your body is for use—not abuse.

Use the bumps in life as stepping-stones.

If you have a small voice, you won't need a big stick.

You can't train a horse with shouts and expect it to obey a whisper.

If things go wrong, don't go with them.

Self-examination is one test from which no Christian is excused.

Discipline should be a delight—not a drudgery.

Real discipline is when you can pick strawberries without eating any.

An ounce of "don't say it" is worth a pound of "didn't mean it."

Discipleship requires discipline.

You can't go crooked as long as you stay on the straight-and-narrow way.

Discipline is the ability to cook a meal without licking your fingers.

The Spirit's keen paring knife enhances a Christian's fruit-bearing life.

Before we have the right to control others, we must learn to control ourselves.

If the going gets easy, you may be going downhill.

To be like the Master, we must learn to master the basics.

Power is the ability to raise your eyebrows instead of your voice.

Sometimes it is harder to keep what you have than it was to get it.

To gain self-control, give Christ control.

Discipline is holy hesitancy.

It's impossible to keep both your mouth and your mind open at the same time.

The straight-and-narrow way would not be so narrow if more people walked on it.

The Christian life is a pilgrim journey, not a sight-seeing tour.

Sometimes love must hurt before it can help.

God cuts away the dead wood to make us fruitful.

Some things your mother told you about . . .

DISCOURAGEMENT

Disappointments should be cremated and not embalmed.

Don't feel discouraged—even the sun has a sinking spell every night, but it rises again in the morning.

A word of encouragement can mean the difference between giving up and going on.

Don't let life discourage you—everyone who got where he is had to begin where he was.

A country mile is the distance between an empty gas tank and the nearest service station.

Disappointments are all God's appointments. Put him between you and your circumstances.

How long will you remain discouraged or frustrated? As long as you choose to be.

You don't have to keep the circumstances someone gave to you.

The difference between encouragement and discouragement is attitude.

Age doesn't change the disappointment of having a scoop of ice cream fall from the cone.

Don't be discouraged—it may be the last key that will open the door.

Disappointment can be God's reappointment.

God uses our setbacks to move us forward.

Some things your mother told you about . . .
DISHONESTY

Sad, but a lie can travel halfway around the world before the truth can tie its shoelaces.

You can always fool others with your words and actions, but you cannot fool yourself.

You cannot practice deception and be right in your heart toward God.

Those who deliberately try to deceive others will deceive themselves.

Regardless of how you may be able to deceive others, you will never deceive God.

A lie has no legs—it has to be supported by other lies.

The best way to spot a counterfeit is to become so familiar with the real thing that you can't be fooled.

It's easy to tell one lie but almost impossible to tell only one.

Two half-truths do not necessarily constitute a whole truth.

A lie is always in a hurry, but truth is willing to wait.

Two things often lead to lying—many promises and many excuses.

When you tell the truth, you have a supernatural power supporting you.

Most things too good to be true aren't.

The reason you can't fool all the people all the time is because some of them are fooling you.

When you get something for a song, watch out for the accompaniment.

Misrepresenting the facts is no different from committing other sins.

The best way to avoid lying is to do nothing that needs to be concealed.

Prefer a loss to a dishonest gain—the one brings pain at the moment, the other for all time.

A false life never goes with a true faith.

Some things your mother told you about . . .

DOUBT

Anxiety reveals a lack of faith.

An anxious person is not a trusting child of God.

Unbelief dishonors God—to please him, we must have faith.

Faith doesn't say, "God can"—it says, "God will!"

Unbelief always stands between you and God's best for your life.

It is the man who has done nothing who is sure nothing can be done.

When someone says, "It can't be done," he is saying, "I can't do it."

A pinch of *probably* is worth a pound of *perhaps.*

Great mountains of happiness grow out of little hills of kindness.

Those who expect nothing in life are never disappointed.

Some things your mother told you about . . .
DREAMS

We cannot dream ourselves into what we could be.

Sitting and wishing will not change your fate—God plans the fishing; you must plan the bait.

We are not put into this world only to dream but also to work out our dreams.

Every dreamer expects to do wonders when he awakes.

Dreaming has its values, but it should never become a substitute for work that needs to be done.

You have to stay awake to make your dreams come true.

A person without a goal will get nowhere and won't know when he gets there.

If you have accomplished everything you planned for your life, you have not planned enough.

People don't understand what you are doing if you really don't know your vision.

Sometimes we look so intently toward the pinnacle that we stumble over the steps leading to it.

Keep your ideals high enough to inspire you and low enough to encourage you.

When you reach for the stars, you may not get one, but you won't come up with a handful of mud, either.

Every field looks greener from a distance.

Dreaming is more than setting a goal—it's doing God's will.

Ideas not put into practice are merely dreams.

Ideas alone won't work—something must be done about them.

Some things your mother told you about . . .

DRINKING

Those who drink much usually think little.

A hangover is something to occupy a head that wasn't used the night before.

When wine enters, wisdom departs.

Alcohol kills the living and preserves the dead.

The hand that lifts the cup of cheer should not be used to shift the gears.

Liquor fools the man who fools with it.

Drinking doesn't drown sorrows—it just irrigates them.

There's nothing wrong with drinking like a fish provided you drink what a fish drinks.

Drinking doesn't drown your sorrows—sorrows know how to swim.

Some things your mother told you about . . .

DRIVING

When in your car, look out for children walking and for children driving.

An automobile is only as drunk as its driver.

If you continue to break the speed limit, be sure your life insurance is up-to-date!

All bad things come to him who goes down a one-way street in the wrong direction.

Don't drive as if you own the road—drive as if you own your car.

Many tombstones are carved by chiseling in traffic.

You may outbluff the other driver, but will you outlive him?

A reckless driver is seldom wreckless for very long.

If you drive carelessly, your car will last a lifetime.

The only speed at which to drive—Godspeed.

Most people use their hands and feet when they drive—a few also use their heads.

The letter S can change a speeding driver from laughter into slaughter.

Drive as if you owned the other car.

Frequent naps prevent old age—especially if taken when driving.

EATING

Face powder may win a husband, but it takes baking powder to keep him.

Many a round figure has been acquired by eating too many square meals.

Gluttony makes the body big and the pocket small.

With small children at the table you get used to whining and dining.

Some things your mother told you about . . .

EDUCATION

The finest education is useless without common sense.

Investment in knowledge pays the best interest.

Reading makes a full man—but what he is filled with depends on what he reads.

Education is what a person gets from reading fine print—experience is what they get for not reading it.

Education should not only train the mind but also the motives and actions.

Never let your studies interfere with your education.

Education should include the knowledge of what to do with it.

Education without God is like a ship without a compass.

Do not entertain ideas—put them to work.

It is not wise to tell everything you know, but it is wise to know everything you tell.

To be conscious that you are ignorant is a great step toward knowledge.

The most dangerous day in any man's life is the day he decides he knows enough.

Those who don't know and don't know they don't know seldom agree with those who do know.

Genius is the gold in the mind; talent is the miner who digs it.

A home without books is like a body without a soul.

Homework is something teenagers do between phone calls.

Education is important, but dedication is more important.

Knowledge is folly unless grace guides it.

Any philosophy that can fit into a nutshell belongs there.

Everyone is a genius at least one time in his life.

Curiosity is the first rung on the ladder of learning.

Those who practice their own teachings are good teachers.

There is no better teaching we may receive than to have God teach us by experience.

God's knowledge is not given to us to boast but to perfect us.

We only hurt ourselves when we refuse to accept God's words of wisdom.

Being proud of your intelligence is a mark of ignorance.

Wisdom will keep you out of trouble, but knowledge is an ongoing learning experience.

Some things your mother told you about . . .
EGO

The person who thinks too highly of himself doesn't think highly enough of Christ.

The man who toots his own horn soon has everybody dodging when he approaches.

Many people fail by falling over their ego.

Some things your mother told you about . . .
ENEMIES

It takes two to make a quarrel—and when one is willing, it's easy to find another.

It takes two to make a quarrel—one can always end it.

He who has revenge in his power and does not use it is a great man.

Revenge may appear to be sweet, but he who indulges in it loses far more than he gains.

A person is mature when he refuses revenge and offers forgiveness.

When seeking revenge, one brings himself down to the level of the one he seeks to get even with.

To do good to an enemy may lose him—as an enemy.

People buy things they don't need to impress people they don't like.

Our worst enemies are not those who hurt us but ourselves when we seek revenge.

It's always possible to learn more from our enemies than we can sometimes learn from our friends.

Show me a person who has never made an enemy and I'll show you a person who hasn't accomplished much.

The time you waste in getting even can be used for getting ahead.

Taking revenge is being equal to your enemy—passing over it makes you supreme.

Revenge gets you even with your enemy; forgiveness puts you above him.

When you dislike a person, do something nice for him.

The only safe way of destroying your enemies is making them your friends.

The hate we feel for our enemies does more harm to our peace of mind than to theirs.

The best way to conquer an enemy is with the weapon of love.

Some things your mother told you about . . .

ENTHUSIASM

Without enthusiasm, nothing very great can be accomplished.

Enthusiasm helps charge the battery of the mind and body.

The worst bankruptcy in the world is the person who has lost his enthusiasm.

Initiative is doing the right thing without being told.

Stop thinking up reasons why something won't work and start thinking of ways that you can make it work.

A barking dog is more useful than a sleeping lion.

You don't feel the splinters on the way up—only when you start sliding back down the ladder.

There is no age to those with enthusiasm.

It is much easier to keep the fire burning than to rekindle it after it has gone out.

A man who is always on the go often never gets there.

The most powerful influence on earth is a soul on fire for God.

Enthusiasm is the yeast that makes the dough rise.

What if you are just a spark? All fires are the same size at the start.

Work done with little effort may yield little fruit.

The sooner you get going, the further ahead you will get.

Those who faithfully get up in the morning will someday get up in the world.

If you don't start, it's certain you won't arrive.

Plan with vision, proceed with optimism, and achieve with enthusiasm.

Some things your mother told you about . . .

EXAMPLE

Don't pretend to be what you don't intend to be.

When people get to know you, will they want to know Christ?

You can preach a better sermon with your life than with your lips.

Every man's work is a portrait of himself.

Five minutes of demonstration is worth more than hours of talk.

Our words may hide our thoughts, but our actions will reveal them.

It is more important to watch how a man lives than to listen to what he says.

It is hard to sell a product you do not use and a religion you do not live.

The most valuable gift you will ever give is a good example.

People may doubt what you say, but they will believe what you do.

Too many people confuse charm with having a good set of teeth.

Live so that when you tell someone you are a Christian, it confirms their suspicions instead of surprising them.

EXAMPLE   85

The best way to prove Christianity is to practice it.

To have integrity is to be good when nobody is looking.

Be careful how you live—you are the only Bible some people read.

A happy heart and joyful actions leave an unerasable example.

So live that when people speak of you, they will think of Jesus.

One example is worth a thousand arguments.

An ounce of practice is worth a pound of preach.

Live the gospel first—tell it later.

The probability that someone is watching you is directly proportional to the stupidity of your action.

Small acts can speak loudly of our faith.

Where we go and what we do advertises who we are.

He who practices what he preaches may have to put in some overtime.

Every time you speak, your mind is on parade.

A man's work is a portrait of himself.

You can't get rid of a bad temper by losing it.

The prayers a man lives on his feet are just as important as those he says on his knees.

The way you teach is important; what you teach is important; how you live is the best way to teach.

People might enjoy us more if we would give as much attention to our behavior as we do to our neighbor's.

The greatest love we can bestow on others is a good example.

If you can see some good in everybody, almost everybody will see some good in you.

Good examples have twice the value of advice.

Don't allow anything in your life you wouldn't want your children to follow.

Only a balanced person is worth imitating.

Today's deeds will be tomorrow's history.

We may teach what we know, but we will reproduce what we are.

How one lives in private will soon emerge in public.

Nothing can dim the beauty that shines from within.

Don't forget that people will size you up by your actions— not your intentions.

What we do may be more important than what we don't do.

Our outward should always be the same as our inward.

One who walks with Christ is a walking sermon.

There isn't any use trying to shine unless you take time to fill your lamp.

We reform others unconsciously when we walk uprightly.

For every benefit you receive, a responsibility comes with it.

You can't measure the depth of the well by the length of the handle of the pump.

When your work speaks for itself, don't interrupt it.

Our words and our deeds should say the same thing.

A quiet testimony is more convincing than a loud sermon.

Without a heart aflame for God, we cannot shine for Jesus.

EXAMPLE 87

Always be on the inside what you profess to be on the outside.

There's a big difference between saying and doing.

Performance will continue to outsell promises.

In public, guard your tongue; in private, guard your thoughts.

Thunder makes much noise, but it is lightning that does the work.

Better is he who does than he who talks about doing.

If Christ is kept on the outside, something must be wrong on the inside.

Reflecting Christ makes us most beautiful.

Works, not words, are the proof of love.

What we leave behind tells how we got ahead.

A wrecked lighthouse is much more dangerous than an uncharted reef.

Some people who think they are bearing their cross are only paying for their mistakes.

A bad example undermines good works.

Imitate those who imitate Christ.

When our lives honor Christ, even silence is eloquent.

You never know when you are making a memory.

An important role we play in life is that of a role model.

When living like Christ, be prepared for people not to like you.

Some things your mother told you about . . .
EXCUSES

If you have a good excuse, don't use it.

Bad men excuse their faults; good men abandon them.

There's a difference between good, sound reasons and reasons that sound good.

Reasons make sense—excuses make nonsense.

Love will find a way—indifference will find an excuse.

Never give an excuse for yourself that you wouldn't accept from another person.

You can never conquer sin with an excuse.

Cooked-up excuses usually sound half-baked.

If half the ingenuity spent in finding excuses were exercised in finding a means, there would be a vast difference.

We can always find a reason for what we do and an excuse for what we don't want to do.

Some things your mother told you about . . .
EXPERIENCE

One thorn of experience is worth a whole wilderness of warning.

Comfort is most effective when it comes from the one who has suffered.

Use the past as a springboard, not as a sofa.

Experience may be the best teacher, but it can't teach an unwilling student.

There is no free tuition in the school of experience.

A new broom sweeps clean—the old broom knows where all the dirt is.

An expert is often a very ordinary fellow away from home.

The average person takes 19,002 steps daily—many of them are in the wrong direction.

The trouble with experience is that just when you think you've got enough—you find out you need some more.

You save yourself the cost of learning from experience when you learn from the experience of others.

If we are wise, we profit from every experience, whether or not it be enjoyable.

An expert is someone who has done something right at least once.

It's better to be a has-been than a "never-was."

A little experience often upsets a lot of theory.

Experience is yesterday's answer to today's problems.

Those who refuse to learn from others will be doomed to learn for themselves.

Every time you graduate from the school of experience, someone thinks up a new course.

Experience is the only thing you can't get on the easy payment plan.

Experience is the looking glass to intellect.

You cannot teach what you do not know nor lead where you do not go.

Yesterday will keep you in bondage so long as it threatens you.

You cannot escape entirely from yesterday, and you should not if you could.

If you had no yesterday, there would be for you no today.

Let yesterday's troubles remain today and you will ruin tomorrow.

progress or decay
it sticks it sneaks out

A Small HINT is worth a TON of Advice

It is bad Manners to talk when your Mouth is full and your Head is EMPTY

F

Some things your mother told you about . . .

FACTS

Fact is fact and feeling is feeling—never does the second change the first.

Facts do not cease to exist because they are ignored.

Facing facts squarely and honestly never harms you.

Some things your mother told you about . . .

FAILURE

Try to fix the mistakes—never the blame.

An admission of error is a sign of strength rather than a confession of weakness.

The archer who overshoots his mark does no better than he who falls short of it.

One person in the whole world can defeat you—you!

It isn't the mountain ahead that wears you out—it's the grain of sand in your shoe.

Defeat isn't bitter if you don't swallow it.

The three hardest words in the English language are "I was wrong."

Admit your mistakes, but don't brag about them.

The man who never makes mistakes loses a great many chances to learn something.

One sure way to fail is to look at your failures.

More people fail through ignorance of their strength than through knowledge of their weakness.

One who doesn't learn from failure will never achieve success.

Failure is no disgrace, but it is a disgrace to do less than your best to keep from failing.

It is no disgrace to acknowledge that we have been in the wrong.

An honest confession is good for the soul.

One way of humbling yourself is to admit you have failed.

The greatest of all faults is to be aware of none.

A fault confessed is half redressed.

Most of our mistakes come from letting our wishes interpret our duties.

Mistakes can and should be growing points in life.

Any man can make a mistake, but only a fool will continue in it.

A small leak will sink a great ship.

It takes only a little soap to make a man slip.

Life's greatest failure is failing to be true to the best you know.

Failure can become a weight or it can give you wings.

Everyone is liable to make mistakes, but fools practice them.

Those who try to do something and fail are better than those who try to do nothing and succeed.

Don't worry when you stumble—remember a worm is about the only thing that can't fall down.

To admit you are wrong is simply to say you are wiser today than you were yesterday.

The failure of men cannot reverse the working of God.

Failure does not mean you will never make it—it means you will have to do it differently.

Be big enough to admit your mistakes, smart enough to profit from them, and strong enough to correct them.

Too many fail because they only stare at the stairs of success.

A fault denied is a fault twice committed.

It is better to ask twice than to lose your way once.

God can use life's reverses to move us forward.

Hurry is the mother of most mistakes.

The way to avoid great faults is to beware of small ones.

It is better to look ahead and prepare than to look back and regret.

Most know the difference between right and wrong—we just don't want to admit it.

We love ourselves in spite of our faults. Why should we not love others in spite of theirs?

The difference between failure and success can be doing a thing nearly right and doing it exactly right.

No one is a failure who can truly say, "I have done my best."

An error is like a leak in the roof—the amount of damage it can do depends on how fast you fix it.

To gain spiritual strength we must acknowledge our weakness.

Sometimes the best gain is to lose.

If you stumble twice on the same stone, you deserve to fall.

Error often wears the disguise of truth.

You will not stumble over mountains, but watch out for those molehills.

No experiment is a failure—you can always use it as a bad example.

Failure happens to those who are afraid to try again.

When success turns a person's head, he's facing failure.

Little mistakes often make great lessons.

Admit your mistakes before someone else exaggerates them.

Some are approximately right but end up precisely wrong.

When you fall down, pick something up.

If you don't want to end in failure, be sure to begin with God.

Don't wait until you are flat on your back before you look up.

A person with a green thumb could either be a gardener or a sloppy painter.

Forget your mistakes, but remember what they taught you.

God can use life's setbacks to move us ahead.

It is better to make a mistake going forward than to make a mistake going backward.

Some things your mother told you about . . .

FAITH

One's faith never accumulates from laying it away in cold storage.

When your faith gets into the past tense, it becomes pretense.

The best way to prove your faith is not to argue about it but to prove it by your actions.

To put more heart into your faith, you must have more faith in your heart.

If your faith costs little, it is worth little.

Let your faith not be a goad but a goal.

There is nothing colder than frozen faith.

Some are inoculated with small doses of faith, preventing them from catching the real thing.

Faith sees a way when reason would despair.

Faith gives no heed to what it sees and feels but stands upon God's Word.

Faith untried may be true faith, but it is likely to remain little as long as it is without trials.

A feeble faith is better than a mighty feeling.

The hand that guides the universe surely is able to handle our little cares.

Great peace comes to those who allow God to take charge of all their cares.

Remember that the faith that moves mountains always carries a pick.

Sensible men think big but start small.

Faith is a way of walking—not a way of talking.

Every day something is being done that couldn't be done.

True faith obeys without doubt or delay.

God may delay or deny our request, but he will never disappoint our trust.

Does your faith move mountains, or do mountains move your faith?

A good commentary on faith is action.

Idle faith is as useless as idle words.

Putting your faith in the living God takes the fear out of living.

You start going down when you stop looking up.

Faith either moves mountains or tunnels through them.

Faith's answer to the question "How?" is one word—"God!"

Faith does not eliminate foresight.

Faith enables us to stand that which we cannot understand.

Great delusions are sometimes taken for great faith.

Faith has an impact upon our behavior.

Faith is God's antidote for fear.

Giving stimulates a growth in your faith.

What God promises, God will provide.

Our work is to care—God's work is to take care.

When you look out, it may be night; when you look up, it's always light.

A faith that has not wept is a faith untried.

The faith of a home—not its wealth or its address—is the foundation of life.

It's much easier to keep the faith if you use it more.

Remember in the dark what God has told you in the light.

Faith is somewhat like a wheelbarrow—you have to put real push behind it.

You need not be afraid of where you're going when you know God is going with you.

Faith is believing what God says simply because it is God who says it.

Ordinary people of faith can do extraordinary things for God.

Troubles will cause you to use or lose your faith.

Large asking and expectation on our part honors God.

If you never stick out your neck, you will never get your head above the crowd.

If you refuse to scale the mountain, you can't enjoy the view.

No person is responsible for the rightness of his faith but only for the uprightness of it.

Keep the faith and keep it simple.

Faith does not depend on what you know but on whom you know.

Do all you can and trust God to do what you cannot.

The faith to move mountains is the reward of those who have moved little hills.

You have never tested God's resources until you have attempted the impossible.

A bridge uncrossed is like a life never lived, a door never opened, a gift never given, a love never shared.

Shadows fall behind when we walk toward light.

Faith makes the uplook good, the outlook bright, the inlook favorable, and the future glorious.

If you want to launch a big ship, you have to go where the water is deep.

Faith needs exercise to grow.

Trust God to move your mountain, but keep on digging.

Faith is the link that connects our weakness to God's strength.

Truly great people never lose their childlike faith.

It is better to walk with God by faith than to go alone by sight.

Faith finds windows—doubt finds walls.

The secret of coping is hoping in God.

Put your faith in Christ and put your fears to rest.

Trust everything to faith.

The creed you really believe is not spoken by your lips but by your life.

Faith is not a leap in the dark but a step into the light.

It's impossible to be neutral in your faith.

There's a big difference between keeping your chin up and sticking your neck out.

Faith always has work to do.

It is better to be poor and walk by faith than to be rich and walk by sight.

Some things your mother told you about . . .

FAITHFULNESS

When you do your work faithfully, your faith will be seen in your work.

The most difficult tasks can be performed if we remain faithful.

The greatest ability is dependability.

True greatness consists in being great in little things.

Great endurance is essential to great achievement.

Work in terms of years, not in the tyranny of days.

Nothing will give you more free time than being on time.

When faithfulness is most difficult, it's most necessary.

Faithfulness in little things is a big thing.

Faithfulness to God results in divine blessings.

It's better to be faithful than famous.

The highest reward for our work isn't what we get but what we become by it.

When you sow the seed of God in faith, don't be concerned who does the reaping.

We are judged by what we finish, not what we start.

Part-time faith, as a part-time job, will not fully support you.

Trusting God's faithfulness dispels our fearfulness.

The example of faithfulness speaks louder than words.

Some things your mother told you about . . .

FAMILY

Family matters matter to God.

The right temperature at home is maintained by warm hearts—not hot heads.

Other things may change us, but we start and end with family.

The family that works together, aches together.

Children may close their eyes to advice, but they open their eyes to example.

Training a child to follow the straight-and-narrow way is easy for parents—all they have to do is lead the way.

A room hung with pictures is a room hung with thoughts.

Children tend to rise to the level of their parents' expectations.

A model family can make a house into a model home.

Families that pray together stay together, and families that work together—eat!

Memories are a family album filled with images and dreams.

The family is the one safe island in an unknown sea.

Wrinkles are hereditary—parents get them from their children.

When you teach your son, you teach your son's son.

Govern a small family as you cook a small fish—very gently.

The child's first school is the family.

The factory that produces the most important product is the home.

Some things your mother told you about . . .

FATHERS

A father is someone who explains how things work and makes you want to be as smart as he is.

The father who puts Christ in his life sets a proper model for children to imitate.

A father holds his children's hands for a while, but he holds their hearts forever.

Any man can be a father, but it takes a special man to be a dad.

The best fathers not only give us life but also teach us how to live.

Many an excellent father is tempted to forget that the best offering he can make his children is himself.

Earthly fathers should reflect their heavenly Father.

Good fathers not only give us life—they teach by example how to live.

Some things your mother told you about . . .

FEAR

If anything can bring your fears to pass, it is your worries.

Fear of failure is the father of failure.

Fear is unbelief parading in disguise.

Fear tends always to produce the thing it is afraid of.

If you rest in the Lord, fear will not keep you from sleeping.

We need not fear shipwreck when Jesus is at the helm.

Those who fear God need not fear death.

The tragedy of today is not so much the noisiness of bad people, but the silence of good people.

Fear brings more pain than does the pain it fears.

Beware lest you lose the substance by grasping at the shadow.

To take fear out of living, put your faith in the living God.

The fear of God can deliver you from the fear of man.

The greatest of our fears shows us the littleness of our faith.

Do the thing you fear and the death of fear is certain.

Fear is the little darkroom where negatives are developed.

Fear God and all other fears will disappear.

The one thing worse than a quitter is the person who is afraid to begin.

When you fix your eyes on God, your fears will vanish.

Fear leaves us when we remember Jesus is with us.

When fear knocks at your door, let faith open it.

Peer pressure is really fear pressure.

Silence is not always golden—sometimes it's guilty.

The right kind of fear prompts us to do right.

Fear creates little worlds and little souls.

Some things your mother told you about . . .
FLATTERY

Flatterers are like cats—they lick before they scratch.

Flattery is the art of telling people exactly what they think of themselves.

There is a short distance between a pat on the back and a kick in the rump.

Flattery is what you say to a person's face that you wouldn't say behind his back.

Some things your mother told you about . . .
FORESIGHT

It may be a long way to your goal, but the next step toward the goal is within reach.

Nothing of importance is ever done without a plan.

Live each day so that you will neither be afraid of tomorrow nor ashamed of yesterday.

It's better to look ahead and be prepared than to look back and regret.

Do not worry about whether or not the sun will rise—be prepared to enjoy it.

Don't follow the crowd—go where there is no path and make a trail.

There is a light for you straight ahead, but you must keep your eyes open to see it.

If you don't know where you are going, any road will get you there.

Some things your mother told you about . . .

FORGETTING

To be wronged is nothing unless you continue to remember it.

Train your mind to forget everything that isn't worth remembering.

A good memory is fine, but the ability to forget is the true test of greatness.

When the danger is past, God is often forgotten.

It's good to forgive—it's better to forget.

The heart holds things the mind forgets.

Forgetfulness is the heart's forgiveness.

There are three types of memory—good, bad, and convenient.

Some things your mother told you about . . .

FORGIVENESS

God does not forget the sinner—he forgives the sinner.

Forgiveness is an eraser that removes ugly blots from the pages of life.

When you are wronged, don't do what comes naturally; do what comes supernaturally.

Forgiveness is when you leave Dad's saw out in the rain and he says it was rusty anyway.

When you bury the hatchet, don't leave the handle sticking out.

Sin brings fear—confession brings freedom.

The greatest of all freedoms is the forgiveness of sin.

Forgiveness heals the wound—forgetting heals the scar.

It is usually easier to forgive an enemy than a friend.

Love not only gives, it also forgives.

For forgiveness to flower, the weeds of bitterness must be uprooted.

Forgiveness is the glue that can repair a broken relationship.

Forgiveness is the key that opens the door to freedom from resentment.

It is better to forgive and forget than to resent and remember.

Two people cannot hate each other if both love God.

If slighted, slight the slight and love the slighter.

It is manlike to punish but Godlike to forgive.

It takes two to make up after a quarrel.

Since we all need forgiveness, we should always be forgiving.

Don't burn a bridge you may have to cross someday.

Confession opens the door to forgiveness.

An apology can be the superglue of life.

Seek to have a hand that gives and a heart that forgives.

When it seems you can't forgive, remember how much you've been forgiven.

When God stops forgiving us, we can stop forgiving others.

Christ is the reason for living and forgiving.

Forgiveness by God removes sin and restores the soul.

A forgiving spirit opens the way to better things.

Some things your mother told you about . . .
FREEDOM

Freedom is not the right to do as you please but the liberty to do as you ought.

Too many are clamoring for the freedom to do what should not be done.

You are free to make your choices but not free to determine the consequences.

Some things your mother told you about . . .

FRIENDSHIP

A good neighbor doubles the value of a house.

If you want to look tall, choose short friends.

A person is sometimes controlled by the company nobody knows he's keeping.

Go often to the house of your friend, for weeds choke up the unused path.

No lifetime is too long to live as a good friend.

No matter how many friends you have, you always have room for more.

Friendship is like money—easier made than kept.

The best saving you will ever do is to save friends.

A true friend will remember your birthday but will forget how many you've had.

If you want people to love you, listen carefully to a lot of things you already know.

Never let competition destroy companionship.

You can withdraw from your friendship account only to the extent of your deposits.

Real friends are those who, when you make a fool of yourself, don't think you've done a permanent job.

It is not *what* you know or *whom* you know that is important, but how you relate to those you know.

It takes a long time to grow an old friend.

Be careful about lending money to a friend—it may damage his memory.

Your brother may not be a friend, but every true friend is a brother.

Every time a man builds a wall around himself he does two things—he walls others out and walls himself in.

It's better to be alone than to be in bad company.

The contact of every human personality is for a divine purpose.

True friends have hearts that beat as one.

A friend is someone who can see through us and still enjoy the show.

Friendship is like a lifeboat in a stormy sea of despair.

You make more friends by showing an interest in people than by trying to get them interested in you.

Many kinds of fruit are grown on the tree of life, but none so sweet as friendship.

The happiest miser on earth is one who saves friends.

Friends are made by many acts but can be lost by one.

Be slow in choosing a friend—slower in changing.

A true friend will not let you stand alone.

Friendship consists of forgetting what one gives and remembering what one receives.

When you're in a jam, a good friend will bring you bread and peanut butter.

A friend is a person who listens attentively while you say nothing.

Wounds from a friend are better than kisses from an enemy.

Friendship fills up all those little ruts in life's road.

True friends are mathematical—they divide sorrows and multiply happiness.

Be as friendly to the janitor as you are to the chairman of the board.

To have a friend, you must be one.

True friendship is like sound health; the value of it is seldom known until lost.

Christ's friendship prevails even when human friendship fails.

Friends are imperfect people who put up with each other's imperfections.

God adds to the beauty of his world by creating true friends.

A good book—like a good friend—is always there in time of need.

To get the most out of a relationship, put all you can into it.

A good neighbor is one who smiles at you over the fence but doesn't try to climb over it.

Get acquainted with your neighbor—you might like him.

It's amazing how nice people are to you when they know you are going away.

Just knowing you have friends who would help is sometimes all the help you need.

A friendship true is like pure gold—it won't wear out because it is old.

We flatter those we scarcely know and please our fleeing guest, but render many a heartless blow to those we love the best.

Before borrowing money from a friend, it's good to decide which you need the most.

Treasure is not always in a friend, but a friend is always a treasure.

Avoid associating yourself with people who never smile.

Friends are those rare people who ask how we are and then wait to hear the answer.

A true friend overlooks your failures and is patient with your success.

Only your true friends will tell you when your face is dirty.

A friend who does not oppose you when you are wrong is not a friend.

Do not use a hatchet to remove a fly from your friend's forehead.

Choose your companions with care—you may become what they are.

A friend doubles a man's joy and cuts his sorrow in half.

A true friend is someone who is there at the drop of a tear.

Friends are the chocolate chips in the cookies of life.

Only as we are on the level with our fellowman can we climb the heights with God.

Don't worry about knowing others—make yourself worth knowing.

When you do a favor for a friend, forget it—when a friend does a favor for you, remember it.

A friend thinks of you when others are thinking of themselves.

A false friend and a shadow remain only when the sun shines.

A false friend has honey in his mouth and gall in his heart.

A false friend is worse than an open enemy.

Tell me who your friends are, and I'll know your character.

A friend is someone who doesn't punch you in the nose, though you've got it coming!

A true friend knows when to speak and when to listen.

When someone you love becomes a memory, the memory becomes a treasure.

A real friend is someone who will visit you on a hot day when you don't have air-conditioning.

Treat your friends like family and your family like friends.

A friend understands what you are trying to say, even when your thoughts aren't fitting into words.

Friendship is a plant we must water often.

A true friend is your most valuable possession.

Some things your mother told you about . . .
FUTURE

It's not where you are, but where you're going.

The future is that time when you'll wish you'd done what you aren't doing now.

The trouble with the future is that it usually arrives before we're ready for it.

Today's footprints are tomorrow's pathways—be careful where you step.

Forget yesterday, enjoy today, welcome tomorrow.

Looking ahead is what keeps us from falling behind.

One generation plants a tree, and the next ones enjoy the shade.

If you haven't figured out where you are going, you're lost before you start.

Go as far as you can see, then you will see further.

To enjoy the future, accept God's forgiveness for the past.

A man has much faith in the future when he plants shade trees that he knows he will never sit under.

Don't let the future scare you—it's just as shaky as you are.

Those who fear the future are likely to fumble the present.

Don't ever count your chicks before they cross the road.

Just over the hill is a beautiful valley, but you must climb the hill to see it.

Tomorrow is a vision waiting to be captured.

You have to be tough to hang on to your dreams.

Don't miss the present by focusing too much on the future.

Dig your well before you are thirsty.

Remember the past, catch the present, believe in the future.

The future belongs to those who create it.

The pull of the future is just as important as the push of the past.

The best way to prepare for tomorrow is to concentrate on doing today's work superbly.

Today is the fruit of yesterday, the seed of tomorrow.

No need to fear the darkness of tomorrow if you're walking in God's light today.

The one who lives for this life only will have eternity to regret it.

Today's preparation determines tomorrow's achievement.

All the flowers of tomorrow are the seeds of today.

Treasures in heaven are laid up only as treasures on earth are laid down.

What you do with Christ now will determine what he will do with you later.

The time to prepare for tomorrow is today.

The good we do today becomes the happiness of tomorrow.

Now is the time to invest in eternity.

What we believe about the world to come shapes how we live in the world today.

Settle all accounts today; you can't bank on tomorrow.

What the future has in store for you depends upon what you have stored for the future.

The future often comes unannounced.

No one can walk backward into the future.

The regrets of yesterday and the fears of tomorrow are the thieves who rob us of today.

The best thing to save for a rainy day is an umbrella.

It's better to have a hen tomorrow than an egg today.

Feeling tense about the future? Remember that God is always present.

You can be confident about the future if you walk with God in the present.

The future is ahead—not behind—you.

The future is not in the hands of fate but in ours.

One who plants a seedling has others besides himself in mind.

We all live under the same sky, but it's interesting how many different horizons there are.

What we sow today determines what we reap tomorrow.

It's never too soon to plan for eternity.

Why we are here is important; where we are going is more important.

GAMBLING

The best way to throw dice? Throw them away.

Those who gamble with their money will gamble with their soul.

GENEROSITY

Generosity does not come naturally—it must be taught.

The hand that gives, gathers.

The Lord notices not only what we give but what we have left.

Don't only give till it hurts—give till it feels good.

If you train a child to give pennies, when he is old he will not depart from it.

God loves a generous giver and a gracious receiver.

Sacrifice is the true measure of generosity.

The greatest pleasure in life is to do a good turn in secret and discover it by accident.

The giver is always in the heart of the receiver.

Giving is an exercise that makes a healthy heart.

Generosity is giving more than you can; pride is taking more than you need.

You make a living by what you get; you make a life by what you give.

Generosity is more charitable than wealth.

There's a difference between charity and giving away what you no longer want.

The finest gifts are the ones we tie with our heartstrings.

Some things your mother told you about . . .

GIVING

The highest kind of giving is done from the bottom of the heart.

It is not necessary to have great wealth in order to give cheerfully.

One who honors the Lord gives him his substance as well as his sentiment.

The more we give, the more we live.

The heart grows rich by giving.

Giving cheerfully is the evidence of genuine love.

True stewardship involves not only our tithes but our offerings as well.

The problem with our giving is that we give the widow's mite without the widow's spirit.

If you want to be rich, give; if you want to be poor, grab; if you want abundance, scatter.

Give your best and the best will come back to you.

Those who give most are least concerned about returns.

Each day is a gift from the one who knows exactly what we need.

Givers always gain.

You give little when you give of your possessions—it is when you give of yourself that you truly give.

Even if you have nothing else to give, you can always give encouragement.

Some things your mother told you about . . .

GOD

No one knows the grace of God who does not know the fear of God.

Safety is not the absence of danger but the presence of God.

You may forget God, but he will never forget you.

To see God in everything can make everything an adventure.

God often empties our hands in order to fill our hearts.

God without man is still God—man without God is nothing!

There are limits to man's love but not to God's.

Communion with God is a daily walk—a nightly watch—a steadfast fellowship.

We worship a God who is greater than our greatest problem.

In a world of many superlatives, God is the greatest.

Nothing is great without God, and nothing is small with God.

People are candles of light, lighted by God to light the lives of others.

If God be your portion, make your plans big.

Think more of what God has done for you than what you feel you have to do for him.

Man may keep away from God, but no one can keep God away from man.

The best way to face life's changes is to look to the unchanging God.

God can take the place of anything, but nothing can take the place of God.

Some people think God is like medicine—you do not need him when you are well.

God's wrath comes by measure, his grace without measure.

To serve a just God involves being servants of God's justice.

God came to dwell with man that man might dwell with God.

God is our authority—not the majority.

To know that God sees us brings both conviction and comfort.

God always stands between the Christian and the enemy.

The heavenly Father's pain became our eternal gain.

He who seeks God will find goodwill.

The light of God's grace shines brightest against the darkness of sin.

God's grace can save the best of sinners as well as the worst of sinners.

Only God's unchanging love can change man's sinful heart.

Anyone can count the seeds in an apple, but only God can count the apples in the seed.

There is no failure more disastrous than the success that leaves God out.

God sees us as we can be but loves us as we are.

If God could speak through a donkey, there's no excuse for anyone to say they cannot speak for God.

We should love God—not just the things he gives us.

The God who holds the universe is the God who is holding you.

Knowing about God is not the same as knowing God.

To reflect God's light, don't seek to be the limelight.

God makes no mistakes. If you think he does, you are mistaken.

Don't tell God what to do—ask him.

A life lived for God leaves a lasting legacy.

To love God is to obey God.

A friend of God will be a stranger to the world.

Every person is precious to the Lord.

Many people believe in God, but not many believe God.

Some see God only in the forest—others see him in every individual tree.

All creation is an outstretched finger pointing toward God.

Never worship the creature more than the Creator.

To be rich in God is far better than to be rich in goods.

God is as great in minuteness as he is in magnitude.

People who have a heart for God have a heart for people.

If we use God's name loosely, we're taking God too lightly.

Fear God and you'll have nothing else to fear.

God wants to be everything to every one of us at every moment.

What you think of God determines what you think of others.

To walk with God, we must talk with God.

We cannot always understand God, but we can always trust him.

God who knows all, sees all, will take care of all.

The best plans begin and end with God.

Troubles seem smaller when you remember the greatness of God.

God likes surprises. Breaking a mold is his specialty.

Some things your mother told you about . . .

GOD'S PROVISION

God knows how weak we are, how foolish we act, and how little we are able to bear.

One cannot drift beyond the love and care of God.

God feeds the birds, but he does not throw the food into their nests.

If I understand that every situation carries a blessing, then today will offer me comfort.

God loves us the way we are, but he loves us too much to leave us that way.

What is over our heads is under God's feet.

No one is poor who can by prayer open the storehouse of God.

When the world around you is crumbling, God is the rock on which you can stand.

God will either lighten our load or strengthen our backs.

He who plants weeds must not expect to gather flowers.

When God bolts the door, don't try to get through a window.

God has provided for today's needs today—tomorrow's needs will be met tomorrow.

What God promises he will provide.

God is stronger than our strongest foe.

Grace means everything to those who deserve nothing.

Our assurance rests more on God's love in our hearts than the logic in our heads.

God made you as you are in order to use you as he planned.

We may ask questions of God, but never should we question what God says.

You have proved the sufficiency of God only when you have trusted him for the impossible.

It is not a question of who you are or what you are but of whether or not God controls you.

God did not call us because we were holy; rather, he called us to make us holy through his workmanship.

Only when you try the impossible do you test the resources of God.

God gives his best to those who leave their lives in his hands.

It is just as easy for God to do a difficult thing as an easy thing.

God develops spiritual power in our lives through pressure in hard places.

The difficulties of life are intended to make us better, not bitter.

Christ died to save us—he now lives to keep us.

True freedom is not in choosing your own way but in yielding to God's way.

A crisis cannot break the one who relies on God's strength.

God is never in a hurry, but he's always on time.

God's grace keeps pace with whatever we face.

God may lead you around, but he'll always lead you aright.

The best motivation to live for Christ is remembering his death for us.

God gives his strength to those who recognize their weakness.

Trusting in God's power prevents panic.

God's clock is never slow, but ours is often fast.

God's offer is a guarantee, not a gamble.

God takes heed to our every need.

With God behind us and his arms beneath us, we can face whatever lies before us.

God's grace can change prodigal sons into profitable saints.

Stumbling blocks may be carved into stepping-stones.

God doesn't always smooth the path, but sometimes he puts springs in the wagon.

Banking on God earns heavenly interest.

It is not how troubled the sea is that determines the course of your life; it is who the pilot is.

What God orders, he pays for.

If God only gave you as much time as you give him, how long would you live?

It's wonderful what God can do with a broken heart if he gets all the pieces.

When God's answer is negative, his reason is affirmative.

Christians who act like beggars have forgotten that God is their Father.

God doesn't use an answering machine—he takes each call personally.

God is more interested in making us what we ought to be than in giving us what we think we ought to have.

If God is your copilot, you had better change seats.

God can use life's stops to keep us going.

God's store never has empty shelves.

Most of the best comes not all at once, but a little at a time.

We judge people by their appearance; God judges them by their motives.

God's help is only a prayer away.

With God's Word as your map and his Spirit as your compass, you're sure to stay on course.

God can bring beauty out of ugly situations.

God's call to a task includes the strength to complete it.

Beautiful flowers are the smile of God's goodness.

God's mercy makes heroes out of zeroes.

God has an all-seeing eye—and an all-forgiving heart.

To make it in a tough world, keep in touch with God.

God always provides what he promises.

Some things your mother told you about . . .

GOSSIP

Gossip has a way of saying nothing that leaves nothing unsaid.

There is nothing busier than idle rumor.

There is a big difference between a "busybody" and a "busy body."

Gossiping and lying go hand in hand.

Don't have more secrets than you can carry yourself.

When it goes in the ear and out the mouth, it's gossip.

Idle gossip keeps some people very busy.

Beware of gossip—it is verbal cyanide!

Plastic surgeons nowadays can do almost anything with the human nose—except keep it out of other people's business.

Gossip is like a scorpion—it is primarily composed of a long tale with a nasty sting.

Don't expect others to keep your secrets if you don't do it yourself.

Busybodies never have anything to do.

Gossip is anything that goes in one ear and over the back fence.

Trying to squash a rumor is like trying to unring a bell.

He who gossips to you will gossip about you.

Gossip travels faster than overnight mail.

Gossip is like a cinnamon roll—good for the tongue, bad for the heart.

Some things your mother told you about . . .

GRACE

Grace humbles a man without degrading him and exalts him without inflating him.

A heart full of grace is better than a head full of notions.

During the darkest of sin, God's grace shines brightest.

Some things your mother told you about . . .
GRATITUDE

He who forgets the language of gratitude can never be on speaking terms with happiness.

Develop an attitude of gratitude.

Be grateful for what you have—not regretful for what you don't have.

Be grateful for the doors of opportunity—and for friends who oil the hinges.

Some things your mother told you about . . .
GRANDPARENTS

Nothing makes a child as smart as having grandparents.

The simplest toy for a child to control is his grandparent.

A grandmother is a mother who has been given a second chance.

Some things your mother told you about . . .
GRUDGES

The heaviest load any man carries on his back is a pack of grudges.

Resentment becomes a black, furry, growing grudge.

No matter how long you nurse a grudge, it won't get any better.

The longer you carry a grudge, the heavier it becomes.

progress only when
it sticks its neck out

A small HINT is worth a TON of Advice

It is bad Manners to talk when your Mouth is full and your Head is EMPTY

H

Some things your mother told you about . . .

HABITS

Clean habits always lead to a clean life.

Serious trouble comes when New Year's resolutions collide with the old year's habits.

Men's natures are alike—it's their habits that make them different.

Choose the best life—habits will make it pleasant.

Do not blame God for the harvest when you, yourself, do the sowing.

The power of a good habit is as great as that of a bad one.

A bad habit is first a caller, then a guest, and at last a master.

You can't sow bad habits and reap a good character.

Good habits are the soul's muscles—the more you use them, the stronger they become.

The worst boss anyone can have is a bad habit.

Today's tendency is tomorrow's custom.

Habit is like a cable—each day we weave a thread and soon we can't break it.

Master your habits, or they will master you!

Practice makes perfect—be careful what you practice.

Some things your mother told you about . . .

HAPPINESS

Happiness consists as much in what you are as in what you have.

Misery may love company, but happiness always has parties.

Don't constantly seek happiness—keep busy and you'll find it.

Happiness is somewhat like trouble—the more you nurse it, the bigger it gets.

Happiness is found not in reward but in honorable effort.

A good thing to have up your sleeve is your funny bone.

Happiness is not having what you want but wanting what you have.

Happiness does not come from getting as much as it does from giving.

If you would truly be happy, seek to make others happy.

People are never too poor but often too rich to be happy.

Happiness is always more enjoyable when you share it.

Happiness is hiring a baby-sitter who is on a diet.

Happiness is like potato salad—when you share it with others, it's a picnic.

Real happiness is the interest we get from our investment in the kingdom of heaven.

No one ever became happy by seeking happiness.

If you seek happiness for yourself alone, you will seek in vain. If you seek to make others happy, you will find happiness.

Happiness is the result of being too busy to be miserable.

The surest steps toward happiness are the church steps— tread them often.

It is not happy people who are thankful, but thankful people who are happy.

Happiness is having an extra pair of shoelaces handy when your laces break.

There are two essentials to happiness—something to do and someone to love.

The Lord's presence can make his people happy in a dungeon.

Happiness is like your shadow—run after it and you will never catch it, but keep your face to the sun and it will follow you.

Do something every day to make someone happy, even if it means leaving them alone.

Shed your thimble psychosis—let your cup run over.

If you learn to laugh at yourself, you will always have something to make you happy.

Sometimes we miss happiness by looking too far for things nearby.

Laughter is the shortest distance of happiness between two people.

Grief can take care of itself—to get more out of happiness, it must be shared.

Very little is needed to make a happy life.

Good humor is goodness and wisdom combined.

Cheer up—birds have bills, but they sing anyway.

Money can bring happiness if you know where and how to shop.

Happiness comes not from having much to live on but from having much to live for.

Use your wit to amuse, not to abuse.

Fun is like insurance—the older you get, the more it costs.

Happiness adds and multiplies as we divide it with others.

The most important thing you wear is a cheerful expression.

A long face shortens your list of friends.

The wag of a dog's tail shows the happiness in his heart.

Cheerfulness will open a door when other keys fail.

Happiness is a conscious choice, not an automatic response.

Happiness is not a station you arrive at but a manner of traveling.

Those who bring sunshine to the lives of others cannot keep it from themselves.

Happiness is not perfected until it is shared.

When you feel terrific, notify your face.

Recall it as often as you want. A happy moment never wears out.

Happiness is good health and a poor memory.

A bad joke is like a bad egg—all the worse for having been cracked.

Happiness is going on vacation without the children.

Cheerfulness is the window cleaner of the mind.

Happiness held is a seed—happiness shared is the flower.

People lose many laughs by not laughing at themselves.

Happiness is putting all your "egos" in one basket—the wastebasket.

The shortest path to your own happiness is the roundabout way of making others happy.

Happiness is stepping on a scale and finding you've lost five pounds.

A cloudy day is no match for a sunny disposition.

Happiness is having your teenage children thank you for your advice.

Unless we find beauty and happiness in our backyard, we will never find it in the mountains.

Happiness is seeing a double chin and an added fifteen pounds on your spouse's old flame.

Happiness is a way of life that makes the most of opportunities, the least of difficulties, and the best of everything.

Happiness often sneaks in through a door we didn't know we'd left open.

Happiness is seeing your children get a job and earn a living on their own.

True happiness of your life depends upon the wholeness of your thoughts.

Happiness is having something interesting to do, someone to love, and something to look forward to.

Happiness: a handy little habit to have around.

The secret of happiness is to count your blessings while others are adding up their troubles.

One way to be happy ever after is not to be after too much.

Happiness is the conviction that we are loved in spite of ourselves.

A small house can hold as much happiness as a big one.

The three archenemies of happiness are hurry, worry, and doubt.

Happiness is like honey—you can pass it around, but some of it will stick to you.

A merry heart is good medicine with no bad side effects.

Happiness is having the principal of the school call, saying how *good* your child has been.

Happiness is making a mistake when there is no one around to notice it.

Some things your mother told you about . . .

HEALTH

A healthy mind is a most valuable asset.

Spiritual health is as important as physical health.

The flu is just a bad cold with a good press agent.

A wonder drug is a drug you wonder if you can afford.

Good health is always above wealth.

There's health and goodness in the mirth in which an honest laugh has birth.

Health is wealth—and it's tax free.

Some things your mother told you about . . .

HEAVEN

Earth is our inn—heaven is our home.

Life with Christ is an endless hope—life without Christ is a hopeless end.

On the road to heaven we must observe the "no boasting" signs.

To believe in heaven is not to run away from life; it is to run toward it.

If you are interested in the hereafter, remember that the *here* determines the *after.*

Aim at heaven and you will get earth thrown in—aim at earth and you will get neither.

A happy Christian home is a foretaste of heaven.

Enjoy life, but anticipate heaven.

When you are in tune with heaven, you'll have a song in your heart.

Some things your mother told you about . . .

HOLINESS

Holiness is not only coming out from the world—it's being different from the world.

Holiness is wholeness—the whole of Christ in the whole life.

Love will endure when you keep it pure.

Keeping away from the mire is better than washing it off.

Your sanctification is like riding a bike—either you keep moving or you will fall down.

If your Christian life is a drag, worldly weights may be to blame.

Being peculiar does not make one holy, but being holy does make one peculiar.

We may cleanse our hands, but only God can cleanse the heart.

Clean living causes funeral homes to wait longer for their money.

Holiness is becoming the person that God wants us to be.

Never attend any activity you cannot invite Christ to attend with you.

We can be in the world without the world being in us.

Always avoid what dulls your sense of sin.

Those who follow the crowd soon get lost in the crowd.

You cannot talk dirty, think dirty, and act dirty, and remain clean.

If there is righteousness in the heart, there will be beauty in the character.

A child of the King shouldn't live like a slave to the world.

Holiness is not a virus to be caught; it's a way of life to be sought.

Loose conduct can get you into tight places.

All the water in the ocean cannot sink a ship unless the water gets into the ship.

God asks us to be holy, not omniscient.

Some things your mother told you about . . .
HOLY SPIRIT

The Holy Spirit is the voice that whispers in your ear from somewhere within your heart.

We don't need more of the Spirit; the Spirit needs more of us.

The Holy Spirit's unction will affect our everyday function.

Some things your mother told you about . . .
HOME

Dry bread at home is better than roast beef in a restaurant.

The home may lose popularity, but there will never be a substitute place to eat corn on the cob.

Home is where our feet may leave, but not our hearts.

A house is not a home unless it has food for the soul as well as the body.

No nation is better than the home life of its people.

Loving homes don't just happen—they're built.

Home is where a person goes after he is tired of being nice to people.

Always leave home with loving words, for they may be the last.

Homes are cleaner today than they were a generation ago. The reason is that they are not used as much.

A home is a house with a heart inside.

Home is where they understand you.

Christian homes don't just happen—they're planned.

A dream home is a house that costs more than you dreamed it would.

Work daily in making your house into a home.

If you behave better in one place than in another, let that place be at home.

A well-groomed park without people is like a clean house without company.

A guest sees more in an hour than the host sees in a year.

One may search all over the world to find what he needs, only to return home to find it.

A home is the father's kingdom, the mother's world, and the child's paradise.

Home is the place where our stomach gets three meals a day and our heart receives a thousand.

A garage sale is a sign you have a house without an attic.

When love adorns the home, other decorations are secondary.

Home is where you hang your memories.

What's in your home mirrors what's in your heart.

A house is made of bricks and stone, but a home is made of love alone.

A house is built with human hands, a home by human hearts.

To have the warmth of Christ's love in your home, let him kindle a fire in your heart.

The true home has no boss, but it does have at least one wise leader.

Disagreements are normal in a home, but quarrels should never occur.

Just about the time they plan to retire, some parents discover that the birds who left the nest are homing pigeons.

A full cabin is better than an empty castle.

The size of a house has nothing to do with how happy it is inside.

A real home is a picture of heaven on earth.

Some things your mother told you about . . .

HONESTY

No one knows of your honesty unless you give out some samples.

If you are not honest with God, you won't be honest with others.

Honesty is not only telling the truth—it's living the truth.

The badge of honesty is simplicity.

A liar is one who has no partition between his imagination and his information.

There are no degrees of honesty.

There is no legacy as rich as integrity.

If you can't get it honestly, don't seek it.

One thing we can give and still keep—our word!

No one passes the man who travels the straight and narrow.

It takes a really honest person to know the difference between when he's tired and when he's just lazy.

He who will be true to God will be true to others.

Innocence is better than repentance.

Honesty is the best policy but difficult to follow in a letter of recommendation.

Nobody ever got hurt on the corners of a square deal.

Honesty means never having to look over your shoulder.

A "square person" is one who is well rounded.

No sincere person will intentionally seek to lead others astray.

Honesty pawned is never redeemed.

Always telling the truth means you have to remember less of what you have said in the past.

You will never go wrong doing right.

Honesty is the first chapter in the book of wisdom.

Our main concern is to do what's right, not what other people think is right.

It is easier to be honest with others than it is to be honest with yourself.

Crime's story would likely be shorter if the sentences were longer.

Honesty may be the best policy, but insanity is a better defense.

Integrity is its own reward.

Better to be an honest atheist than a false Christian.

Some things your mother told you about . . .

HOPE

No one is hopeless whose hope is in God.

What appears to be the end may really be a new beginning.

No life is hopeless unless Christ is ruled out.

The secret of coping is hoping—in God.

The ladder of hope has nothing to stand on here below; it is held from up above.

Sunset in one land is sunrise in another.

The blue of heaven is larger than the clouds.

Correction can help—but giving hope can help more.

Hope is faith going places.

Only when we walk in the dark do we see the stars.

If you feel low and down—remember the sun goes down each night, but it rises in the morning.

You may be on top of the world, but remember, it turns over every twenty-four hours.

Hope is a good anchor, but it needs something to grip.

You will find the sunshine if you search for it.

We should cling to old memories but have young hopes.

There are no hopeless situations—only people who have lost hope.

All is not hopeless when your hope is in God.

Christ is the difference between hope and hopelessness.

Hope in the heart puts a smile upon the face.

The sun is always shining somewhere.

Hope is like the sun—sometimes it shines, sometimes it goes under, but it never goes away forever.

Some things your mother told you about . . .
HUMILITY

Humility begins by kneeling at the cross—continued humility requires the same.

Knowing Christ makes us humble; knowing ourselves keeps us humble.

If you are willing to admit you're all wrong when you are, you're all right.

There's nothing wrong with starting at the bottom—unless you're learning to swim.

Only a lamb has the grace to suckle kneeling.

There are two kinds of people—those who are humble and those who are about to be.

If you don't learn humility, you will learn humiliation.

Exalt yourself and you'll never be close to God—humble yourself and he will descend to you.

Humility puts us where God can bless us and fit us for service.

Meekness is not weakness but strength under proper discipline.

Humility is the root of all heavenly virtues.

Other people can break your spirit, but only you can humble yourself.

The well digger is the only person who can start at the top and go down.

In Christian service, the branches that bear the most fruit hang the lowest.

If you cannot be the highway, just be the rail.

If you think meekness is weakness, try being meek for a week.

A humble talent that is used is worth more than genius that is idle.

The man who kneels to God can stand up to anything.

Meekness is the strength to back down from a fight you know you could win.

If you think you are too small to do a big thing, try doing small things in a big way.

If God had wanted us to pat ourselves on the back, he would have given us hinges.

People who do things that count never stop to count them.

Sometimes it's better to dance in the wings than to be center stage.

You should ask God for humility but never thank him that you've attained it.

Humility is that precious quality that makes us feel smaller as we grow greater.

You must be melted before you are molded.

Many would be scantily clad if clothes were their humility.

Broken things become useful in God's hands.

A humbled heart will lead to callused knees.

The more we bury our ego, the more fruit we bear.

Standing tall for Christ means stooping to help others.

Second fiddle is one of the most difficult instruments to play.

To learn to walk humbly, begin on your knees.

Humility is honest self-appraisal.

Humility is being teachable.

When you are swept off your feet, slip down to your knees.

No matter how high the bird flies, he must come down for water.

Nothing is so hard to do gracefully as to get down off your high horse.

Self-demotion will bring God's promotion.

Christ is seen most clearly when we remain in the background.

You have to be little to belittle.

Those God greatly exalts he first humbles.

It is better to bend with the breeze than to snap when a strong gust comes along.

Those who have the right to boast don't have to.

When someone else blows your horn, the sound carries twice as far.

Humility can be sought but never celebrated.

A good man is always willing to be little.

Some things your mother told you about . . .
HUMOR

If you're laughed at, don't worry—a comedian makes a living at it.

People who read the comics first in the morning live longer than those who read the obituaries.

Humor is hazardous to your stress.

A sense of humor is like a needle and thread—it will patch up many things.

Some things your mother told you about . . .
HUSBANDS

A husband who thinks he's smarter than his wife is married to a very smart woman.

No woman likes a perfect husband, because it doesn't give her anything to do.

The wise husband meets a marital crisis with a firm hand—full of candy and flowers.

The smart husband never asks who is boss around the house.

The smart married man is the fellow who convinces himself he likes to wash dishes.

To be a good husband, learn to say in a dozen words what the wife can say in a thousand.

The best way to remember your wife's birthday is to forget it once.

It's all right to forget your wife's birthday, if you forget which one it is.

The smart husband thinks twice before speaking.

To see how patient your husband is, watch him fish.

Never look for a worm in the apple of your wife.

To have an ideal wife you must be an ideal husband.

Getting a husband is like buying a used car. You don't see it like it is but like it's going to be when you get it fixed up.

If you seek a model husband, be sure he is a working model.

Never yell at your wife unless the house is on fire.

The best way to compliment your wife is frequently.

To be a diplomat you must be able to bring home the bacon without spilling the beans.

Some things your mother told you about . . .

HYPOCRISY

The best acting at the Academy Awards is done by the losers congratulating the winners.

A sickly saint often resembles a healthy hypocrite.

A hypocrite has God in his mouth and the world in his heart.

A hypocrite is someone who complains there is too much sex and violence on his VCR.

Hypocritical piety is double iniquity.

A fool who speaks the truth is better than a hundred liars.

Some things your mother told you about . . .

IGNORANCE

Ignorance is not hereditary—it's acquired.

Unread books make empty heads.

Ignorance does not kill you, but it makes you sweat a lot.

Little things affect little minds.

Why is it that the fewer the facts, the stronger the opinion?

He who jumps to conclusions cannot always expect a happy landing.

Never trust a man who wears blue socks with a brown suit.

When the majority agree on an idiotic idea, it is still an idiotic idea.

Nothing is more dangerous than a big idea in a small mind.

It's easy to count those who can't count to ten—they are in front of you in the supermarket express line.

Unless you are willing to admit your ignorance, you will never acquire knowledge.

Ignorance of wrongdoing does not make one innocent for having done wrong.

An impartial observer is somebody who doesn't know what's going on.

What you don't know may not hurt you, but it may make you look pretty stupid.

A person's mind may be broad but have no depth.

You never get too old to learn something foolish or to do something stupid.

One thing about ignorance—it causes a lot of interesting arguments.

The more you know, the more you know you don't know.

Never forget that you are a part of the people who can be fooled some of the time.

The emptier the pot, the quicker it boils.

Blooming idiots have no off-season.

The only person more stupid than the person who thinks he knows it all is the person who argues with him.

Ignorance combined with silence sometimes is mistaken for wisdom.

The worst ignorance is an ignorance of God.

To be conscious that you are ignorant is a great step toward knowledge.

A fool is as smart as everyone else as long as he keeps his mouth shut.

A narrow mind plus a wide mouth means equals trouble.

It's easy to prove a fool is wrong—let him have his way.

A good idea can get very lonely in an empty head.

Fools pursue pleasure regardless of the cost.

Shallow rivers and shallow minds are the first to freeze over.

The problem with ignorance is that it picks up confidence as it goes along.

Some things your mother told you about . . .
INDIFFERENCE

Lofty doctrine and low practice do not go well together.

It is no use to be fervent in spirit if you are not fair in business.

Regardless of your profession of Christ, if there is not a change in your lifestyle, you are not truly a Christian.

Much charity that begins at home is too weak to travel.

A willful waster is a woeful wanter.

If you stand still and watch the world go by, it will.

The mice are always bold when the cat is absent.

You cannot attain eminence by climbing on the fence.

A rut differs from a grave only in depth.

A man who doesn't have a leg to stand on is always a pushover for a fellow with both feet on the ground.

Little things are like weeds—the longer we neglect them, the larger they grow.

Distrust a shallow religion.

Many aim at nothing and hit it with remarkable precision.

There are two kinds of Christians—those who wait on the Lord, and those who make the Lord wait on them.

The straight-and-narrow path never crosses Easy Street.

Life may begin at forty, but you will miss a lot if you wait until then.

The deaf or earless soul will not hear the voice of God.

Thinking too long about doing something often becomes its undoing.

The Lord prepares a table for his children, but too many are on a diet.

Luck is what shallow minds believe in.

More tools are ruined by rust than by overuse.

The greatest wastes are unused talents and untried ideas.

Unless you are the lead dog, the scenery never changes.

If you skate on thin ice, you'll end up in hot water.

Caution is not cowardly, and carelessness is not courage.

If you want to remain where you are in life, never do more than you have to do.

It is difficult to steer a parked car, so get moving.

Only a mediocre person is always at his best.

It takes little effort to watch the other person carry the load.

A second-class effort never produces a first-class result.

Some things your mother told you about . . .
INFLATION

Just about the time you think you can make both ends meet, someone moves the ends.

Inflation is when nobody has enough money because everybody has too much.

Some things your mother told you about . . .
INSULTS

Some people are experts at handing out baloney disguised as food for thought.

The truest test of moral courage is the ability to ignore the insult.

A small HINT is worth a TON of Advice

It is bad Manners to talk when your Mouth is full and your Head is EMPTY

J

Some things your mother told you about . . .

JEALOUSY

If you shoot arrows of envy at others, you wound yourself.

Envy provides the mud that failure throws at success.

Very few can stand prosperity if it's in the other fellow.

Envy is an open door to bitterness.

Envy is always ready to spoil any happiness.

Envy is counting someone else's blessings instead of counting your own.

Jealousy is a passion that ruins the character and personality of anyone who has it.

When you feel yourself turning green with envy, you are ripe for trouble.

Being overcome with envy is like running into the ocean—the deeper you go in, the harder it is to get out.

Some things your mother told you about . . .

JESUS

Jesus is the believer's rest, the believer's peace, and the believer's security.

Balance the bad news of life with the good news of Christ.

One who is not humbled in the presence of Jesus does not know him.

Follow Christ and you will lead others to him.

Though Christ was born in the first century, he belongs to all centuries.

The love of Christ is the only sure antidote for the love of money.

A wise man will not only bow at the manger but also at the cross.

The Lamb who died to save us is also the Shepherd who lives to lead us.

Jesus is God spelled out in language that man can understand.

Jesus is the only physician who can cure his patients by taking their disease.

What you decide about Jesus determines your destiny.

Christ is the only way to heaven; all other paths are detours to doom.

The surest way to drive out darkness is to bring in the Light.

He is not alone who is alone with Jesus.

To win Christ is the greatest gain.

When your outlook is blurred by problems, focus on Christ.

Jesus came to save the lost, the last, and the least.

Jesus became what we are so we could become what he is.

Unless Christ is the center of interest, your life will be out of focus.

Jesus didn't wear a cross—he bore it!

Be sure you know Jesus as Savior before you face him as judge.

If you don't like the way the cookie crumbles, try the Bread of Life.

Jesus is the bridge over troubled waters.

Jesus is the rock that doesn't roll.

It isn't what you know about Jesus that counts; it's what you do with him.

Jesus is not a reformer—he's a redeemer.

Jesus is at his best when we are at our worst.

The Bread of Life never becomes stale.

Some things your mother told you about . . .

JOY

Don't expect to enjoy life if you keep your milk of human kindness all bottled up.

One joy dispels a hundred cares.

Happiness depends on happenings—joy depends on Jesus.

Joy is not the absence of suffering but the presence of God.

Satisfaction is the soil where joy survives.

Joy is the by-product of trusting God.

The joy you give to others keeps coming back to you.

Unshared joy is an unlighted candle.

The greatest joy on earth is the sure prospect of heaven.

Joy is spiritual prosperity.

Some things your mother told you about . . .

KINDNESS

Wherever there are people, there are opportunities for kindness.

Wise sayings may be forgotten but kind words never are.

A kind word helps keep discouragement away.

He that has not kindness has not strong faith.

Kindness begets kindness.

No one ever regrets being kind.

Don't expect to have a good life if you fail to show kindness.

You can kill anger with kindness.

Speak kindly today; when tomorrow comes, you will be in better practice.

Even a tombstone will say good things about a fellow when he is down.

Speak kind words and you'll hear kind echoes.

One visit is worth more than a card, phone call, or fruit basket.

True kindness is loving others more than they deserve.

Knowing the Golden Rule is good but not as good as practicing it.

A little kindness can make a big difference.

Warm weather is nice, but a warm heart is better.

You will be happier if you give people a piece of your heart instead of a piece of your mind.

Kind words never wear out the tongue.

The more good we find to say about a person, the more good that person will become.

Charity begins at home and generally dies from a lack of outdoor exercise.

The kindly word that falls today may bear fruit tomorrow.

Nothing is so strong as gentleness—nothing so gentle as real strength.

He who sows courtesy reaps friendship, and he who plants kindness gathers love.

Politeness is a small price to pay for the goodwill and affection of others.

A little oil of courtesy would eliminate a lot of friction.

Gentleness helps us make a point without making an enemy.

Do unto others as though you were others.

A kind word is better than a large meal.

You will be sorry for speaking a harsh word but never for speaking a kind word.

A heart closed to the gospel may be opened by a helping hand.

The best gifts are always tied with heartstrings.

The way we treat our neighbor is the way we treat God.

We grow a little every time we do not take advantage of somebody's weakness.

You can never do kindness too soon, for you never know when it may be too late.

Never return kindness—pass it on.

Thoughtful words and loving deeds help to fill empty lives.

Kind actions begin with kind thoughts.

It doesn't take a lot of muscle to give the heart a lift.

People need love—especially those who don't deserve it.

Christians should pray for a tough skin but a tender heart.

There are no unimportant jobs, no unimportant people, and no unimportant acts of kindness.

One little act of kindness is better than feelings of love for all mankind.

The best thing to do behind a person's back is to pat it.

Consideration for others means taking a wing instead of a drumstick.

Guard within yourself the treasure of kindness. Know how to give without hesitation, how to lose without regret, and how to acquire without meanness.

You can't love everyone, but you can be kind to everyone.

True kindness warns and rescues.

People, like refrigerators, need defrosting occasionally.

When you pass out the milk of human kindness, don't skim it.

Kindness is never out of season.

Kindness is like snow—it will make beautiful anything it covers.

Every charitable act is a stepping-stone toward heaven.

To get out of a hard situation, try a soft answer.

It's not true that nice guys finish last. They are winners before the game ever starts.

A soft answer has been the means of breaking a hard heart.

The best way to knock a chip off your neighbor's shoulder is a pat on the back.

In labors of love, every day is payday.

You can measure a person's worth by the size of his heart.

People take heart when you give them yours.

Timely good deeds are nicer than afterthoughts.

The milk of human kindness never curdles.

A kind heart is the fountain of gladness.

Kindness is in the hand more than in the heart.

It's easy to care when you share.

Gentleness and kindness will conquer in the end.

Kindness is the chain that holds society together.

Search others for their virtues and yourself for vices.

He that demands mercy and shows none ruins the bridge over which he himself is to pass.

Gentleness—you don't kill a flea with a cannon.

The Good Samaritan doesn't wait for the media to arrive before he does his thing.

Fragrance lingers on the hands of those who hand out roses.

Carve your name on hearts—not marble.

Some things your mother told you about . . .

KNOWLEDGE

Those who feel they know the most often know the least.

Happy is he who knows error and lets it alone.

Find new and better ways of doing the old job.

Knowledge has no power until it's used.

Knowledge is useless unless common sense accompanies it.

Knowledge that is not put into practice is useless.

Knowledge without wisdom is a course of trouble in life.

Knowledge is power when it is turned on.

No matter what happens, there is always someone who knew it would.

You have to know the ropes in order to pull the strings.

Knowledge is one thing that doesn't become secondhand when used.

Cleverness does not take the place of knowledge.

Some people drink deeply at the fountain of knowledge—others only gargle.

L

Some things your mother told you about . . .

LAUGHING

Laugh and the world laughs with you; cry and you'll feel better.

A laugh is worth a thousand groans.

The person who laughs loudly usually cries loudly.

Laugh and the world laughs with you; snore and you sleep alone.

He who laughs last probably wanted to tell the story himself.

Laughter is a tranquilizer with no side effects.

Wholesome laughter has great face value.

What we laugh at reveals our character.

If you're to be able to look back on something and laugh about it, you might as well laugh about it now.

Laughter is the sunlight of the soul.

Clean the cobwebs out of your heart with a hearty laugh.

Some things your mother told you about . . .
LAZINESS

It takes some people a long time to get nothing done.

When some people are asked to do some charity work, they will stop at nothing.

Idleness is evil in itself and the parent of almost every kind of sin.

He who works is tempted by one devil—he who is idle by a thousand.

Idleness travels so slowly that poverty soon overtakes it.

Too many are ready to carry the stool when there's a piano to move.

People who speak by the yard and move by the inch should be moved by the foot.

Leisure is a good garment, but if it is used too often, it wears out.

Laziness won't disappear—you must work it off.

Those who do nothing in particular eventually become very good at it.

The only thing that sat its way to success was a hen.

It doesn't do any good to sit up and take notice if you keep on sitting.

Some things your mother told you about . . .

LEADERSHIP

The attitude of the leader determines the attitude of the followers.

You cannot lead anyone farther than you have gone yourself.

The world turns aside to let any man pass who is sure where he's going.

He who ceases to learn cannot adequately teach.

Do not ask others to go where you will not lead.

True leaders daily practice faith, fidelity, and faithfulness.

The direction we move in is more imporant than where we stand.

A good leader is a good servant.

You must be willing to follow if you expect God to lead.

A good leader not only knows the way but shows the way.

Lead or follow, but don't complain.

A good leader is someone who takes a little more than his share of the blame and a little less than his share of the credit.

Every leader needs to look back once in a while to see if he has any followers.

Some things your mother told you about . . .
LEARNING

A learned man always has wealth within himself.

Learning is something no one can ever steal from you.

It's impossible for people to learn what they think they already know.

The simplest things are the hardest to grasp—like a bar of soap in a bathtub.

Those who feel they can learn from everyone are truly wise people.

It's never too late to learn, but we often learn too late.

It's what you learn after you know it all that really counts.

No one is ever too old to learn, but many put it off.

Some things your mother told you about . . .
LIFE

In the race of life, it's always too soon to quit.

Life is like a book—the further you get into it, the more it begins to make sense.

Don't wait for the bus at the train station.

Life is like a ladder—every step we take is either up or down.

Life lived just to satisfy yourself never satisfies anybody.

All the world is a stage, and most of us need rehearsals.

About the time one learns how to make the most of life, most of it is gone.

It's the little things that matter the most—what good is a bathtub without the plug?

If you fall seven times, stand up eight.

Life is all ups and downs—up in the air or down in the mouth; up to something or down on somebody; up the creek or down in the dumps.

Live your life like a snowfall—leave a mark but not a stain.

Life is too short to dwell on the mistakes of the past.

Never fear getting off the beaten path—there are more flowers there.

A task worth doing and friends worth having make life worthwhile.

It's not life's chances but choices that bring happiness.

The shortest distance between two points is usually under construction.

Life is only boring when it has no purpose or goal.

Life is short—eat dessert first.

It isn't what you have but what you are that makes life worth living.

Life is a one-way street, and you are not coming back.

Life is full of checks, and many of them are forgeries.

Life is like a mirror—if you frown, it frowns back. If you smile, it smiles back.

Seek to make life richer for others and you'll find your own life becoming richer.

Life is a road we must all travel whether we like it or not.

The real art of living is beginning where you are.

Half of our lives are spent wishing for tomorrow, the other half wishing for our yesterdays.

Life is like a ten-speed bike—most of us have gears we never use.

Life is like a sandwich—the more you add to it, the better it becomes.

Life offers no obstacles—only challenges.

Make the most of your life before most of it is gone.

Your life is God's gift to you—what you do with it is your gift to God.

Life is hard by the yards—by the inch, it's a cinch.

Learn as though you were to live forever—live as though you were to die tomorrow.

If you find life empty, try putting something into it.

Sometimes what looks like a light at the end of the tunnel is an oncoming train.

Life is easier than you think. All you have to do is accept the impossible, do without the indispensable, and bear the intolerable.

For those who fight for it, life has a flavor the sheltered never know.

One's life: a little gleam of time between two eternities.

Enjoy your life without comparing it with that of others.

Life is as unpredictable as a grapefruit squirt.

Live as if you were required to post your past.

When life becomes all snarled up, offer it to the Lord and let him untie the knots.

The path of life is pleasant, if you stop to think where you are going.

Life is like a rubber band—the harder you pull, the farther you go.

Life's moments are so precious that God gives them only one at a time.

Life is not a problem to be solved but a gift to be enjoyed.

A spendthrift is a person who tries to get more out of life than there is in it.

Life is like a garden—it requires cultivation.

Life is like a game of cards—we can't help the hand that is dealt us, but we can help the way we play it.

Life is too hard to trust no one.

Your life is like a coin. You can spend it any way you want, but you can only spend it once.

Only Jesus can give wholeness of life.

Life is a continuous process of getting used to things we hadn't expected.

Some things your mother told you about . . .

LISTENING

Two good talkers cannot make one good listener.

The head has not heard until the heart has listened.

To hear God's voice, turn down the world's volume.

Always listen to the opinions of others—it may not do you much good, but it will them.

All wise men share one trait—the ability to listen.

More knowledge enters your head through open ears than through an open mouth.

With two eyes and one tongue, you should see twice as much as you say.

Talk is the activity of the mouth; listening is the activity of the heart.

There are times when a quiet listener outshines a brilliant conversationalist.

He who speaks sows—he who listens reaps.

Listening may be the most important thing you do today.

You always win more friends with your ears than with your mouth.

If at first you don't succeed, try looking in the wastebasket for the directions.

It's the simple things in life that make living worthwhile— love, duty, work, rest, and listening to God.

It is better that things go in one ear and out the other than if they go in one ear, get scrambled between the ears, and come out the mouth.

What you hear never sounds half as important as what you overhear.

Some people listen like a worm in a cornfield—in one ear and out the other.

Skillful listening is the best remedy for loneliness and laryngitis.

Help reduce noise pollution—be a good listener.

Some things your mother told you about . . .

LOVE

Love people, not things; use things, not people.

Love compels—love constrains.

One proof of your love is how you handle reproof.

Humans were made to run on love, and they do not function well on anything else.

When love is present, nothing can break the bond of unity.

Heads, hearts, and hands could settle the world's problems better than arms.

A love that will not bear all, care all, and share all is not love at all.

Others will not care how much we know until they know how much we care.

It is better to have loved and lost than to have paid for it and not liked it.

Love encourages as it corrects and gives hope as it reproves.

Anyone can be a heart specialist—the only requirement is loving somebody.

True love is never afraid of giving too much.

You cannot love those you envy.

If men had second sight, there would be fewer cases of love at first sight.

God's love is the same when he wounds as when he heals, when he takes away as when he gives.

God loves you as much in times of trouble as he does in times of happiness.

Sympathy is never wasted except when you give it to yourself.

To be loved is better than to be famous.

Love is a talent all may possess.

No man can lead who does not love the men he leads.

The language of love needs no interpreter.

Love not only makes the world go around, it makes the ride worthwhile.

Love is as warm among peasants as among kings.

Love rules without a sword—love binds without a cord.

Love and eggs are best when they are fresh.

Love is the magical bond where one and one are far more than just two.

No matter how love is invested, it always brings big returns.

Money can't buy love, but it certainly makes shopping interesting.

Love is like measles—worse if it comes late in life.

Love may be blind, but it doesn't stay that way long.

A hug is a perfect gift—one size fits all and nobody minds if you give it back.

Love does not dominate—it cultivates.

Selfishness makes Christianity a burden—love makes it a delight.

Love is like a bridge—cross over it, but don't establish yourself upon it.

Love has converted more sinners than zeal, eloquence, or learning.

Love reduces friction to a fraction.

Real love stories never have an ending.

Age doesn't protect you from love, but love sometimes can protect you from age.

Love is when you make cookies for the church bake sale and then buy them back.

Love is when two people with their eyes shut can see heaven.

Love is oceans of emotions surrounded by expanses of expense.

Love is a sweet dream, and marriage is the alarm clock.

Love is not blind; it just does not tell what it sees.

There are more people who wish to be loved than are willing to love.

The cat and the love you give away always come back to you.

Love is friendship set to music.

Money cannot buy love, but it can put you in a good bargaining position.

When there is love in the home, there is joy in the heart.

Love not only makes the world go around, it makes a lot of people dizzy.

Nothing costs as much as loving except not loving.

Love cannot be perfect if it knows no suffering.

Love is more easily demonstrated than defined.

The heart that loves is always young.

Love always finds a home in the heart of a friend.

Love helps those who may never return the favor.

It's hard to hate someone you pray for.

Some things your mother told you about . . .

MANNERS

Good manners are not inherited.

Beware of overly polite people—they usually want something.

Chivalry is a man's inclination to defend a woman against every man but himself.

Manners is the ability to say, "No, thank you," when you are still hungry.

Politeness is an inexpensive way of making friends.

Politeness is to do and say the kindest things in the kindest way.

Fine eloquence consists in saying all that should be said, not all that could be said.

The test of good manners is being able to put up pleasantly with bad ones.

Politeness is benevolence in small things.

It's bad manners to talk when your mouth is full and your head is empty.

Good manners is allowing others to tell you what you already know.

You can see how important manners are by watching people who don't have any.

The more one uses good manners, the easier it is to keep them polished.

Rudeness is the weak man's imitation of strength.

Some things your mother told you about . . .

MARRIAGE

The most shocked woman is the one who got married because she was tired of working.

The most difficult year of marriage is the one you're in.

It's bad to have a rooster who is silent and a hen who crows.

Successful marriage is a creative achievement.

Love at first sight is easy to understand—after forty years it's a miracle.

A good marriage is like a casserole—only those responsible for it really know what goes into it.

It's more important to be the right person than to find the right person.

Matrimony is the only state that allows a woman to work eighteen hours a day.

A true marriage is a source of many blessings and happiness to each other.

If it weren't for marriage, some would go through life thinking they had never made any mistakes.

On the sea of matrimony you have to expect occasional squalls.

One of the quickest ways to stop believing in dreams—marry one.

Matrimony is the splice of life.

Marriage teaches you loyalty, tolerance, understanding, patience, and many other things you don't learn being single.

A happy wife sometimes has the best husband but more often makes the best of the husband she has.

It takes two to make a quarrel and the same number to get married.

A love nest can be broken up by a lark.

A good marriage requires a determination to be married for good.

The sea of matrimony is filled with hardships.

Marrying for beauty is like buying a house only for the paint.

In marriage, don't expect more than you intend to give.

The wrong kind of puppy love can lead to the doghouse.

In marriage, don't lose your head and heart at the same time.

God created man and woman to complement each other, not to compete with each other.

In marriage, don't launch out into the "sea of matrimony" in an empty vessel.

The difference between a successful marriage and a mediocre one consists of leaving about three or four things a day unsaid.

The marriage certificate is not a certificate of ownership but rather of partnership.

In marriage, don't assume you are the captain—it's a mutual management.

Never marry a person for looks or money—you could lose both.

Do not expect more of your "intended" than you intend to give.

Marrying a comedian does not assure you of a happy marriage.

Some things your mother told you about . . .
MATURITY

There are no shortcuts on the way to spiritual maturity.

Turn horse sense into stable thinking.

Maturity is knowing when to speak your mind and when to mind your speech.

Little minds are wounded by little things.

Our actions and behavior never seem to keep up with our ages.

It's all right for shoes to be half soled, but a man must be whole souled.

Perfection is the bull's-eye of a target that no one has ever hit.

Regardless of how tall your parents were, you need to do your own growing.

Perfection may never be reached—but it's worth reaching for.

You have matured when you have learned to laugh at yourself.

Maturity is the stage of life when you don't see eye to eye but can walk arm in arm.

Growing is a lifetime job, and we grow most when we're down in the valleys with the fertilizer.

Change is inevitable, but growth is optional.

At age twenty we don't care what the world thinks of us. At age fifty we find out it wasn't thinking of us at all.

The mature Christian will be a praying Christian.

Maturity is like a delicious cake—it's homemade.

A lot of maturing takes place between "It fell" and "I dropped it."

Some things your mother told you about . . .

MEN

There are three ships in a man's life—friendship, courtship, battleship.

A boy becomes a man when he walks around a puddle and not through it.

A man's character is what God and his wife know him to be.

The quality of a man's life is in direct proportion to his commitment to excellence.

If you can buy a man's friendship, it isn't worth it.

A man can consider himself an honest man when he does his best—even when no one is looking.

Judge a man by his enemies.

The real hero is the man who is brave when nobody's looking.

One cannot always be a hero, but one can always be a gentleman.

Men are like wine—some turn into vinegar, but the best improve with age.

Some things your mother told you about . . .

MISUNDERSTANDING

Remain silent and some suspect you are ignorant—talk and you remove all doubt.

Don't be disturbed at being misunderstood—be disturbed at not understanding.

There are no such things as weeds—only flowers in the wrong places.

A bright eye indicates curiosity and a black eye indicates too much curiosity.

Some things your mother told you about . . .

MONEY

Economy is a way of spending money without getting any fun out of it.

Prosperity keeps many people in debt.

Be careful if you live in the lap of luxury, because luxury might stand up.

A person's attitude toward God is revealed by his attitude toward money.

No gift is greater than the giver himself.

The Bible does not forbid us from making money—it only forbids money from making us.

One way to reduce blood pressure is to live within your income.

Unless the heart is full, even a rich man is poor.

It's amazing how people give the waitress a 15 percent tip but can't afford to give 10 percent to God.

When a man is poor, he leads a simple life—when he is rich, the doctors order it.

Out of debt—out of danger.

When in debt, someone owns a part of you.

A fool and his money are welcome everywhere.

The one person to watch if you plan to save money is yourself.

A beggar will never be bankrupt.

Even if you have a fifteen-bedroom house, you can only sleep in one room at a time.

Dollars go further when accompanied by sense.

He who works only for money seldom goes far.

A rich man may never find true happiness, but he gets a chance to try all the substitutes.

Nothing can build a man's confidence like a big bank account.

Money doesn't make a man a success—but it sure makes him think he is.

A fool and his money will always have a lot of girlfriends.

The things money can't buy are wonderful, but the things money can buy aren't bad.

When a man is poor, the doctors tell him he's got an itch— if he's rich, he has an allergy.

It's practically impossible for a girl with a rich father to end up an old maid.

A man has reached maturity when he realizes there is no such thing as a friendly loan.

Wealth is a worry if you have it and a worry if you don't have it.

Anyone who thinks there's a shortage of coins hasn't been to church recently.

We like to dream about a million dollars, but we hate to think about all the work it takes to make it.

Money talks but is certainly hard of hearing when you call it.

Money may not bring happiness, but it is nice to find out for yourself.

Money makes fools of famous people, but it also makes famous people of fools.

No matter how much money talks, most people don't find it boring.

It's not a bargain unless you can use it.

Without a rich heart, wealth is an ugly beggar.

A bargain is anything that is overpriced less than it could be.

A man may make money, but money cannot make a man.

Earn all you can; save all you can; give all you can.

Regardless of how much money people may have, they will leave it all when they die.

It used to be that a fool and his money were soon parted, but now it happens to everybody.

The poorest of all men is the one who has nothing but money.

It's a dog's life to spend your whole time in making money.

Lots of people become rich by keeping too busy to spend the money they earn.

The way we use money is a testimony louder than any words.

The hoarding of money can blight the human soul.

The best things in life are free, and the next best are very expensive.

Even if money grew on trees, some people would get most of it.

Live within your income, and you will live without worry and a lot of other things.

He that is extravagant will quickly become poor.

We need not have riches in order to make life rich.

There are two ways to be rich: either have all you want, or want all you have.

A fool and his money are soon spotted.

The only harder thing to keep than a secret is money.

Money can change people as often as it changes hands.

Don't allow your possessions to possess you.

Money buys everything except love, personality, freedom, and immortality.

When money speaks, the truth is silent.

Learn to separate your need from your greed.

A penny saved is a penny earned, but a dollar spent is a buck shot.

A small debt makes a debtor—a heavy one makes an enemy.

Some things your mother told you about . . .
MOTHERS

There is no modern pain medicine as effective as a mother's kiss.

The joys of motherhood are what a woman experiences every day—after the kids are put to bed.

Motherhood is a partnership with God.

Children may leave home, but they will always take their mother's heart with them.

Mothers, as well as fools, sometimes walk where angels fear to travel.

It's not at his mother's knees but across them where a youngster learns his best lessons.

No gift that you give to your mother can compare with the gift that your mother gave you.

Only a mother's love can be divided equally among her children.

The best of all home remedies is a good mother.

An ounce of mother is worth a pound of clergy.

Mothers write on the hearts of their children what the world's rough hand cannot erase.

The best kind of mother-in-law is the woman who remembers she was once a daughter-in-law.

Some things your mother told you about . . .

MUSIC

If playing the piano by ear, be careful not to get your earring caught in the keys.

The leader of the orchestra is always a man who has played second fiddle.

When you buy something for a song, it's good to check the accompaniment.

A bird cannot FLY if it is in the egg

People who JUMP often land on a lie

Some things your mother told you about . . .

OBEDIENCE

To stay in the channel of blessing, follow the course of obedience.

The cost of obedience is small compared with the cost of disobedience.

Obedience is another word for love and loyalty.

We should not seek to improve the gospel—we should simply obey it.

Keep God's commandments and they will keep you.

By obeying, one learns to obey.

To the degree we are willing to obey, God is willing to reveal his will.

The purpose in life is not to find your freedom but your master.

A small step of obedience is a giant step toward blessing.

Obedience is the pathway to joy.

Religious activity is no substitute for an obedient heart.

God will never overrule our disobedience to answer our prayers.

You can never go wrong when you choose to obey Christ.

He who is too big to obey is too small to be obeyed.

Some things your mother told you about . . .
OLD AGE

When you bend over twice to pick up something, you are middle-aged.

If you ache before you get out of bed, you are getting old.

Fun is expensive, and the older you get, the more expensive it is.

Old age is that time when you realize you are not the center of the universe.

We never stop laughing because we are old—we grow old because we stop laughing.

Some things your mother told you about . . .
OPPORTUNITY

Opportunities are like millstones—they can grind your corn, and they can drown you.

God's best gifts to us are not things but opportunities.

Don't wait for opportunity to come—it's already here.

With every opportunity comes the weight of responsibility.

Freedom is not safety but opportunity.

Many fail to recognize opportunity because it is often disguised as hard work.

Great opportunities to help others come seldom, but small ones surround us daily.

If opportunity came disguised as temptation, one knock would be enough.

Small opportunities are often the beginning of great enterprises.

When embracing opportunity, give it a big hug.

Often the hard knocks in life are unrecognized opportunities.

You have only one chance at this life—make every second count.

Learn to listen—opportunity sometimes knocks softly.

Instead of using the words "if only," try substituting the words "next time."

Days are like suitcases—the same size, but some people are able to pack more into them than others.

The best time to do something is between yesterday and tomorrow.

No opportunity is ever lost—someone else seizes the ones you missed.

We can do nothing about yesterday and less about tomorrow, but today we can move the world.

The only doors that matter are those we open today.

Many don't see opportunities until they cease to exist.

Don't overlook life's small joys while searching for the big ones.

When on the right road, all sorts of opportunities open.

He who passes by an opportunity to do good in order to find a better one will search in vain.

The hour of opportunity lies near the hours of prayer.

Opportunity sometimes has to kick a man to wake him up.

Fools occasionally find opportunities, but wise men make them.

The knock on the front door may be opportunity, but it may also be another salesman.

Think of failure as an opportunity to try again, wiser than before.

If God closes one door, he will always open another.

Too many people miss the silver lining because they're too busy looking for gold.

The early bird may get the worm, but the second mouse is the one that gets the cheese.

The door of opportunity doesn't open with a remote control.

When a door opens, don't hesitate to enter.

Rarely miss an opportunity to keep your mouth shut.

If the grass is greener on the other side, you can bet the water bill is higher too.

Every day is new and exciting—unlike TV, there are no reruns.

Some things your mother told you about . . .

OPTIMISM

An optimist is one who is treed by a lion but enjoys the scenery.

You may live in a small house, but you can look out the windows and see the whole wide world.

There is no eyestrain when you look on the bright side of things.

Say the best; think the rest.

There are no bad days—some are just better than others.

No weed can grow where a flower stands.

Correction does much—encouragement does more.

Inhale the positive; exhale the negative.

There may be light ahead, but you will have to keep your chin up to see it.

When it rains, some see only the mud—others see the flowers.

Look what you have left—not what you have lost.

A successful man is one who can lay a firm foundation with bricks others have thrown at him.

Make chariot wheels out of your difficulties and ride to success.

Don't be so open-minded that your brains fall out.

The shortest line is the distance between a baby and anything breakable.

When it rains, look for the rainbow.

progress only when it sticks its neck out

A small HINT is worth a TON of Advice

It is bad Manners to talk when your Mouth is full and your Head is EMPTY

P

Some things your mother told you about . . .

PARENTS

Children live to bless the memory of a true parent.

Children never appreciate parents until they become parents themselves.

Parents are just baby-sitters for God.

Children are influenced more by their parents' character than by their parents' accomplishments.

Parents perform many important functions, including eating what's left in cereal boxes.

Do not allow anything in your life that you do not want reproduced in your children's lives.

To win children, serve with grace and respond with love.

Our children may go wrong if we don't start them right.

Live so that when your children think of fairness, caring, and integrity, they think of you.

Parents never fully appreciate teachers until it rains all day.

The best memory parents can leave for their children is taking time with them.

Don't do anything at home you don't want your children to do in public.

The parents' life is a child's guidebook.

To hold on to your children, you must release them to God.

Parents who are afraid to put their foot down usually have children who step on their toes.

Some things your mother told you about . . .

PAST

Don't let yesterday use up too much of today.

Be warned, guided, and taught by the past; don't become a slave to it.

He who learns nothing from the past will be punished by the future.

Much costly time can be wasted in mourning over sins that God has forgiven.

Once you've looked back, you are ready to move forward.

It does not matter what happened—yesterday is dead.

It's too late to do anything about yesterday, but we can do a lot about today and tomorrow.

Every person shares one thing with the moon—they both have a dark side.

No man is rich enough to buy back his past.

We should strive to preserve the fires of the past, not the ashes.

Nostalgia—life in the past lane.

Sawdust cannot be resawn.

Some things your mother told you about . . .

PATIENCE

Patience is a virtue that carries a lot of wait.

By perseverance the snail reached the ark.

A diamond is a chunk of coal that made good under pressure.

God may stretch your patience to enlarge your soul.

Nonchalance is the ability to remain down-to-earth when everything else is up in the air.

Patience is the healer of all pains.

Pray for a poor memory when people treat you unkindly.

He who waits obtains what he wishes.

The waiting time is the hardest time of all.

Impatience is "waiting in a hurry."

Patience is waiting without worrying.

You are never laid aside by illness; you are called aside to stillness.

The secret of patience is to do something else in the meantime.

The greatest prayer is for patience.

Patience is the ability to let your light shine after your fuse is blown.

Always be patient with others, but also be patient with yourself.

He conquers who endures.

Staying calm is the best way to take the wind out of an angry man's sails.

To love butterflies we must care for caterpillars.

If you must choose between power and patience—make it patience.

Patience is the art of concealing your impatience.

If you are at the end of your rope, keep your feet on the ground.

Before you get to the Promised Land, you have to go through the wilderness.

Take sour grapes with a grain of salt.

If God puts you on hold, don't hang up.

You can't plant a seed and pick the fruit the next morning.

The road of the extra mile is never crowded.

God didn't create hurry.

Every fish bites sooner or later.

Patience may be a bitter plant, but it has sweet fruit.

About the only thing you can get in a hurry is trouble.

Patience: a bird cannot fly when it is in the egg.

Calmness is another word for confidence, and confidence is faith in action.

Have patience—all things are difficult before they become easy.

Giving too much information prematurely will do you more harm than good.

Always maintain a cool head and a warm heart.

A flower has to go through a lot of dirt before it can bloom.

Some things your mother told you about . . .

PEACE

Our hatred of someone does not affect their peace of mind, but it certainly can ruin ours.

To have the peace of God, we must be at peace with God.

Make war with your vices and peace with your neighbors.

In every desert or calamity, God has an oasis of comfort.

Be quiet—you'll like it!

Swords may build a throne, but you can't sit on it!

In the still waters are the largest fish.

Peace is seeing a sunset and knowing whom to thank.

You won't fall when your hand is in the hand of God.

Even when the fabric of peace is carefully woven, a few scraps are always left over.

Christ calls the restless ones to find rest in him.

The rainbows of life follow the storms.

Some things your mother told you about . . .

PERSONHOOD

Every idea has its origin in the mind of a person.

No two people are alike, and both are glad of it.

Whoever you are, there is a place to be filled that only you can fill.

Anyone who looks like his or her passport photo is not healthy enough to travel.

What crops up may not be what we wish we had planted.

Genuine elation comes when you feel you could touch a star without standing on tiptoe.

Don't expect anything original from an echo.

Give less thought to what people are thinking of you, and you will have more time to think well of them.

Give first impressions a second opinion.

Some stones are better left unturned.

There's an advantage to being short—you're the last one to know it's raining.

We always know what to do about something until it happens to us.

Perfect timing is the ability to turn off the hot and cold shower faucets at the same time.

If the only tool you have is a hammer, you will tend to see every problem as a nail.

Though God enables, we must do the work he enables us for.

As soon as you get on easy street, they start tearing up the pavement for repairs.

The real test of class is how you treat people who can't possibly do you any good.

Live so the preacher won't have to lie at your funeral.

Getting back on the right track usually involves getting out of a rut.

The difference between a champ and a chump is *u!*

Respect for God will cause others to respect you.

The same people who roll out the red carpet for you today will pull it out from you tomorrow.

It is a great thing to do a little thing well.

Observe everything—be careful what you admire.

If you want to set the world right, start with yourself.

Don't wait for your ship to come in if you haven't sent one out.

Learn to ride in the engine, not the caboose.

Happiness, freedom, and peace all are attained by giving them away.

If you can't hitch your wagon to a star, push it until you reach the star.

To leave footsteps on the sands of life, you have to be on your toes.

The sunrise should never find us where the sunset has left us.

Lust and reason are enemies.

Your life will produce no shadow as long as you remain in the shade.

Hold yourself responsible for a higher standard than anyone else expects of you.

Slow down—the thing you're rushing to may not be as important as the thing you're passing.

Most people use weak thread when mending their ways.

The human brain is like a freight car—guaranteed to have a certain capacity but often running empty.

Never saw off the branch you are sitting on.

So often we overlook the important while attending to the urgent.

It takes as much energy to wish as it does to plan.

Though God does much for us, he wants to do much through us as well.

If you accept correction, you'll need less of it.

Some people would rather pray for forgiveness than fight temptation.

Everyone believes the Golden Rule—give to others the advice you can't use yourself.

The one thing you can do better than anyone else is read your own handwriting.

Don't only do what you like to do, but learn to like what has to be done.

When you are up to your ears in alligators, it's too late to drain the swamp.

You can never win simply by trying to even the score.

When you are kicking, you have only one leg to stand on.

Overlook the faults of others and overcome your own.

We are not what we think we are, but what we think, we are.

Your feet always seem to follow your heart.

When you have a pet peeve, it's remarkable how often you pet it.

Some things your mother told you about . . .
PESSIMISM

When everything seems to be going right, there's something wrong.

Stop looking at the world through woe-colored glasses.

There are no hopeless situations—there are only men who grow hopeless about them.

You won't leave footprints in the sand if you are a heel.

It is impossible to be prayerful and pessimistic at the same time.

Some things your mother told you about . . .
POLITICIANS

If you can fool most of the people most of the time, you're a successful politician.

A committee is a group that keeps minutes and loses hours.

Some things your mother told you about . . .
POVERTY

The world has been enriched more by the poverty of its saints than by the wealth of its millionaires.

Many wits are sharpened on the grindstone of poverty.

Some things your mother told you about . . .

PRAISE

Hem your blessings with praise lest they unravel.

Praise loudly—blame softly.

Praises come naturally to those who count their blessings.

Praise is great, if you don't use it on yourself.

The Lord never stops giving us reasons to praise him.

Praise does wonders for the sense of hearing.

A pat on the back is miles ahead in results.

Compliments cost nothing, yet many pay a high price for them.

A word of praise is equal to a dose of medicine.

Praise is not massaging God's ego to get him to do things for us.

Praise changes the climate where we live.

Praise beats out hell's brushfire.

Praise is the language of the heart set free.

Some things your mother told you about . . .

PRAYER

Prayer is sometimes the hardest work of all.

If we take God seriously, we'll be serious about prayer.

Some prayers are so long because a person prays for more than he works for.

When we do not pray, we become self-centered, self-sufficient, and self-limited.

Prayer is the key to God's storehouse.

Fervent prayer means you mean business with God.

The world would be a better place if men prayed as hard in church as they do at the gambling table.

Prayer has a boomerang effect—it blesses the one prayed for *and* the one who prays.

We should be thankful to God that not all our prayers are answered the way we think we want.

He who sings prays twice.

True prayer does not require eloquence but earnestness.

You cannot wrestle with God and wrangle with your fellowman.

It's not the number of words that make for true prayer.

Prayer that is mere words never reaches God.

To grow tall spiritually, begin by kneeling.

Prayer is not a last extremity but the first necessity.

Don't make the mistake of praying to God but deciding things for yourself.

God answers prayer but not always in the way we wish.

If we pray in times of victory, we will not need to plead in times of defeat.

When it seems hardest to pray, we should pray the hardest.

An important part of praying is a willingness to be part of the answer.

Mend your nets with prayer, cast them in faith, and draw them in with love.

When life knocks you down to your knees, you are in a perfect position to pray.

Prayer is something more than asking God to run errands for us.

You cannot stumble when you are on your knees.

True prayer is a way of life, not just an emergency route.

Prayer was never intended to be a labor-saving device.

He who tunes up in the morning stays in harmony all day.

Your home should be prayer-conditioned.

You can expect God to intervene if you're willing to intercede.

If we pray to catch the ear of man, we can't expect to reach the ear of God.

Prayer flies where the eagle never flew.

True prayer changes self more than it changes others.

A prayerless Christian is a powerless Christian.

Make it a point to pinpoint your prayers.

To avoid a breakdown, take a prayer break.

Nobody has so little that there is no room for praise or so much that there is no need for prayer.

When we clasp our hands in prayer, God opens his.

Prayer should be more than a wish list.

Do not expect a thousand-dollar answer to a ten-cent prayer.

Prayer does move mountains, but sometimes God hands us a shovel.

Our country was better when people opened their meals with prayer instead of can openers.

The most fervent prayers aren't said on the knees but rather when one is on one's back.

When prayer focuses, power falls.

When you bend your knees in prayer, it keeps you from breaking under the load of care.

Prayer digs the channel from the reservoir of God's boundless resources to the tiny pools of our lives.

Too many people pray for emergency rations instead of daily bread.

Some things your mother told you about . . .

PREACHING

It's all right to have a train of thought as long as you have a terminal in mind.

If it goes without saying, don't say it.

You earn the right to preach by listening.

Stand up to be seen, speak up to be heard, and shut up to be appreciated.

An inch of putting into practice is worth a foot of just preaching about it.

Never hit anything head-on that you can sideswipe.

There are few bad short sermons.

If you can't stand the smell of sheep, don't seek to be a shepherd.

Some things your mother told you about . . .

PREJUDICE

Prejudice is a loose idea firmly held.

Nothing is easier to pick up and harder to drop than a prejudice.

Partiality builds walls; love breaks them down.

A single-track mind is all right if it is on the right track.

To be prejudiced is always to be weak.

Jumping to conclusions is a poor form of exercise.

Prejudice is the child of ignorance.

Some things your mother told you about . . .

PRIDE

It's easy to believe even liars when they are saying nice things about us.

Those who love themselves will have no rivals.

God's blessings are not upon the proud in heart.

A proud person is a foreigner to intimate communion with God.

Boasting of one's strong points is a weakness.

The empty vessel makes the loudest sound.

Boasting is the refuge of those more able to talk than to do.

Boasting is always an evidence of felt weakness.

Better others praise you than you praise yourself.

Always keep your head up, but be careful to keep your nose where it belongs.

If you serve only for the praise of men, you will lose the approval of God.

The person who has the right to boast doesn't have to.

The person who toots his own horn the loudest is generally the one who is in the fog.

People with a lot of brass are seldom polished.

Give some people an inch of authority and they think they are a ruler.

It's good to believe in yourself, but don't be overly convinced.

The steam that blows the whistle can't be used to turn the wheels.

It's impossible to push yourself ahead by patting yourself on the back.

Some folks think that traveling around in the best circles makes them big wheels.

Men who pray much don't bray much.

It doesn't pay to get "stuck up"—remember the peacock today may be a feather duster tomorrow.

He who gets too big for his britches will be exposed in the end.

Turning up one's nose gets it bent out of shape.

If you blow your own horn, people will be quick to get out of your way.

Don't try to impress others—let them have the fun of impressing you.

Some are like the rooster, who thinks the sun rises to hear him crow.

Many people want to be the varnish, few want to be the wood.

Don't criticize the rooster—you would crow, too, if you got up at 4:00 A.M.

Pride is a roadblock on the way to heaven.

Storms of applause are things that wreck many sailors.

Swallowing your pride won't choke you.

Those who feel good about themselves will leave God's presence empty.

The spiritually proud Christian forgets his dependence upon God.

Some things your mother told you about . . .

PROCRASTINATION

If you wait for perfect conditions, you'll never get anything done.

Postponement is the mother of disaster.

Don't try to bear tomorrow's burdens with today's grace.

Putting off an easy thing makes it difficult—putting off a hard one makes it impossible.

Today is seldom too early—tomorrow is usually too late.

It seems the greatest labor-saving device of all time is tomorrow.

You don't get much done by starting tomorrow.

Do not be so busy planning for tomorrow that you have no time to enjoy today's sunshine.

Never put off until tomorrow a kindness you can do today.

Do what good you can today—you may not be here tomorrow.

To get something done, it's only necessary to be half as busy today as you plan to be tomorrow.

If it wasn't for the last minute, a lot of things would never get done.

When you say you will do a job tomorrow, ask yourself what you did about it yesterday.

Start doing today what you wish to do well tomorrow.

Always put off till tomorrow what you shouldn't do at all.

Today is the day to make memories.

The ones who always put off until tomorrow are too lazy for God to use.

Some things your mother told you about . . .

PROMISE

Be slow to make a promise—once you have made it, be in haste to keep it.

Promises made lightly are lightly broken.

It is better to do and not promise than to promise and not do.

Complete your promises with deeds.

He who promises runs into debt.

One thing you can give and still keep is your word.

A promise should be given with caution and kept with care.

The promises most likely to be broken are those we make to ourselves.

Promises are like snowballs—easy to make but hard to keep.

Promises may get friends, but it is performance that keeps them.

A courteous refusal is better than a broken promise.

Some things your mother told you about . . .

QUALITY

Good quality is never cheap; cheap quality is never good.

Quantity is what you can count—quality is what you can count on.

Halfway home never gets you there.

progress onl[...]
i[f] sticks its [n]eck out

A small HINT is worth a TON of Advice

It is bad Manners to talk when your Mouth is full and you Head is EMPTY

R

Some things your mother told you about . . .
REPENTANCE

Reform that you may preserve.

Real repentance is sorrow for the deed—not for being caught.

Repentance is to be sorry enough for sinning that you quit sinning.

There's no use going to the altar to tell God how good you are.

Repentance must never be reduced to self-improvement.

Many seek forgiveness without repentance.

The first step in receiving God's forgiveness is repenting of our sins.

When making a mess, be willing to confess.

Some things your mother told you about . . .

REPUTATION

Your name is something you have that everyone else uses more than you do.

A good reputation, like goodwill, is built up by many actions and may be lost by one.

White lies are likely to leave black marks on a man's reputation.

You may be better than your reputation but never better than your ideals.

It is better to earn recognition without getting it than to get recognition without earning it.

It's better to be trusted than to be loved.

Reputation is not to be valued above character.

Conscience is due to yourself, reputation to your neighbor.

Destroying someone's reputation is as wrong in God's eyes as taking his life.

Some things your mother told you about . . .

RESPONSIBILITY

You should stand up for your rights, but not in an intersection.

There is no right way to do the wrong thing.

Take care of the molehills and the mountains will take care of themselves.

The only thing to do about anything is the right thing.

Be sure you are right, then go ahead—be sure you are wrong before you quit.

Too many people make cemeteries of their lives by burying their talents.

Circumstances make a person neither strong nor weak—they only show which he is.

It is easier to dodge responsibility than it is to dodge the result of irresponsibility.

Everyone is responsible for the light in their lamp.

The narrow road is not a conveyor belt—you have to do all the walking.

Don't let danger deter you from doing your duty.

The load doesn't break you down—it's the way you carry it.

Better late than never, but never late is better.

The price of greatness is responsibility.

Not all gifts are free; some have hidden price tags.

People forget how fast you did the job—but they remember how well you did it.

Duties belong to us; results belong to God.

If you take responsibility upon your shoulders, it will leave no room for chips.

There is a place that only you can fill.

Giving to some people is like giving to chickens—the more you give, the less they will scratch for themselves.

Privilege and responsibility are two sides of a coin.

Some things your mother told you about . . .

RIGHTEOUSNESS

Garments of righteousness will never go out of style.

It is just as important to do the right things as to do things right.

Doing what is right and good doesn't always win the applause of the crowd.

Being right half the time beats being half right all the time.

What is popular is not always right; what is right is not always popular.

Trifles make perfection, but perfection is no trifle.

Some things your mother told you about . . .

ROMANCE

Romance is cooking a gourmet meal—reality is washing all the dishes afterwards.

Love is a four-letter word that can spell trouble.

The moon always sways the tide, and also the untied.

Some things your mother told you about . . .

RUMORS

There is nothing as effective as a bunch of facts to spoil a good rumor.

It is easier to float a rumor than to sink one.

Whenever we fan the flames of a rumor, we are likely to be burned ourselves.

There are no idle rumors—rumors are always busy.

Nothing will stir up more mud than a groundless rumor.

S

Some things your mother told you about . . .

SALVATION

Salvation is not giving up something—it is receiving Someone.

Christ freed us from slavery that we might serve him freely.

Jesus offers us life, even though we caused his death.

Redemption was not an afterthought with God.

Your soul is the greatest thing God ever created.

Grace wipes out the sin but does not erase all the consequences.

Unless one drinks now of the "water of life," he will thirst forever.

It's never too soon to come home to God.

Why pay the high cost of being lost when salvation is free?

The way to prepare to meet God is to live for him now.

Salvation is something that is given—not something that is gained.

You can have tons of religion without one ounce of salvation.

It is better to be saved by a lighthouse than by a lifeboat.

No one is good enough to save himself; no one is bad enough that God cannot save him.

Some things your mother told you about . . .
SATAN

Satan's ploys are no match for the Savior's power.

The devil can wall you around, but he cannot roof you in.

There are no losers with Jesus and no winners with the devil.

The devil gratifies—God satisfies.

The devil is a better theologian than any of us and is a devil still.

Satan's place should be under our feet—not on our back.

If the devil can catch a person idle, he will quickly put him to work.

Some things your mother told you about . . .
SCHOOL

If you must fall in love during the school year—do it on weekends.

Don't get mad at your father and mother. Remember,

you just have to attend classes; they have to go to PTA meetings!

Some things your mother told you about . . .

SELF-AWARENESS

Before seeking to change the world, be sure you are willing to make a personal change.

Those who make the biggest impact for God first allow God to make an impact on them.

The vision to see, the faith to believe, and the will to do will take you anywhere.

Even a short pencil is better than a short memory.

What we see often depends on what we are looking for.

So often we seek a change in our condition when what we need is a change in our attitude.

The light that shows us our sin is the light that heals us.

No secret is harder to keep than your opinion of yourself.

To stay away from heels, stay on your toes.

When you have to swallow your own medicine, the spoon always seems too big.

Beware of pride, prejudice, and partiality.

People who live in glass houses have to answer the doorbell.

Get your soul in tune with God before the concert of the day begins.

God cannot meet your need until you feel your need.

Mind your business before someone else does.

The best way to better your lot is to do a lot better.

Fifty-one percent of being smart is knowing what you are dumb at.

Conquering ourselves is harder than conquering a mountain.

Change yourself and your work will seem different.

Use your weakness as a strength—never your strength as a weakness.

The person who trims himself to suit everybody will soon whittle himself away.

What is swept under the rug usually has a way of coming out the other side.

The noble secret of laughing at oneself is the greatest humor of all.

Everyone has an equal chance to become greater than he is.

You must be willing to play the game—no one ever keeps the score of referees.

When you are in a hole, stop digging.

Don't spend the last half of your life regretting the first half.

A mirror doesn't lie, and thank God it doesn't laugh.

You may improve your looks and fool Mother Nature, but you'll never fool Father Time.

When you put a limit on what you will do, you put a limit on what you can do.

Before you can move the world, you must move yourself.

Don't talk about yourself; it will be done when you leave.

If things are not coming your way, perhaps you are going in the wrong direction.

If you could kick the person who causes you the most problems, you couldn't sit down for a month.

The quickest way to acquire self-confidence is to do what you are afraid to do.

You can find yourself by finding God.

None of us will ever be perfect, but we can all be better.

Of all the things you wear, your expression is the most important.

If life deals you lemons, pucker up and get ready to be kissed.

We need so little; the problem is we often want too much.

If you say you are less than you are, people will think you are wiser than you are.

Don't ask questions unless you are willing to accept the answers.

Some feel that holding on makes you strong—sometimes strength is in letting go.

Lessons to the educated can sometimes come from the least educated people.

Every donkey thinks himself worthy to stand with the king's horses.

Regardless of the sound, all birds love to hear themselves sing.

Before desiring it, deserve it.

The sign of strength is to admit you don't have all the answers.

What you are tomorrow depends on what you do today.

Admit you are wrong and you'll be all right.

Make your point, but don't stick anyone with it.

Prepare for the worst—hope for the best.

Clearing away the cobwebs does no good unless you get the spider.

Most of the mountains we climb in this life we build ourselves.

What we prevent needs no cure.

Improvement begins with "I."

Blessed are the flexible, for they shall not get bent out of shape.

Great ideas need landing gear as well as wings.

Learn to relax without feeling guilty.

Asking God for miracles is no substitute for using God-given means.

A bad attitude is like a flat tire—you'll never go anywhere until you fix it.

We cannot always change the circumstances in our lives, but we can change our attitude toward them.

Never underestimate your ability—others will do that.

You may have doubts, but never doubt yourself.

The mirror always tells the truth, but the viewer interprets the reflection to suit himself.

Some things your mother told you about . . .

SELF-DENIAL

Jesus always carries the heavy end of the cross.

Blessings always come through cross bearing.

To wear a crown in heaven, we must bear our cross on earth.

It is better to undertake a large task and get it half done than to undertake nothing and get it all done.

The crowns we wear in heaven must be won on earth.

The path of self-denial is the way to peace of heart.

Christ's yoke is lined with love.

Let a pig and a boy have everything they want, and you'll get a good pig and a bad boy.

Dying to self produces life.

It's better to suffer for the cause of Christ than for the cause of Christ to suffer.

Nothing can be obtained from nothing.

Look at God through your difficulties and you will see him a long way off—look at your difficulties through God and you will not see them at all.

School yourself by self-denial if you wish to be master of self.

The first lesson in Christ's school is self-denial.

To be a crown bearer in heaven will mean being a cross bearer on earth.

Young fools, if not careful, grow up to be old fools.

Nothing is more pleasing to God than self-sacrifice.

Some things your mother told you about . . .

SELF-ESTEEM

Don't let what you can't do interfere with what you can do.

Until we have proper respect for ourselves, we'll never have respect for others.

What you are determines your worth.

Don't think why you can't—think how you can.

Self-confidence is acceptable only if it is rooted in God-confidence.

Keep in step with yourself and you need not worry about the rest of the parade.

You are just as good as anybody else but not a bit better.

You are the only one who can use your ability.

The first step in anything new is having confidence in yourself.

You'll accomplish far more by focusing on your abilities instead of your limitations.

The minute you settle for less than you deserve, you get even less than you settled for.

Never look down—you may miss a rainbow or a sunbeam.

No one can make you feel inferior without your consent.

Some things your mother told you about . . .

SELFISHNESS

The emptiest package in the world is a man all wrapped up in himself.

Most of our problems are created by wanting things we don't really need.

One becomes his full self only by becoming an instrument of a cause that is greater than himself.

The person who shouts the loudest for justice generally wants justice in his favor.

Live only for yourself, and soon you will find there isn't much worthwhile to live for.

A self-pitying life will soon be a doomed life.

Guard against selfishness as you would any serious illness or accident.

Self-pity diseases the soul and destroys all backbone and poise.

Self-pity is an advanced form of selfishness.

One who lives only for himself has not yet begun to live.

Those who walk on the stilts of self-righteousness find it difficult to kneel.

No one will ever do us as much harm as we do to ourselves.

There is nothing noble in being superior to other people.

True nobility is being superior to your previous self.

Anything you are determined to get that you don't need has you in its possession.

The person all wrapped up in himself is overdressed.

Selfish people always lose more than they gain.

Nobody wins when we play favorites.

We do not play the game fair if we deliberately set out to get more than we give.

Living only for temporal gain is sure to bring eternal loss.

A person is never so empty as when he is full of self.

The more we serve Christ, the less we will serve self.

Pain is inevitable—self-pity is optional.

He who gets something for nothing should not complain about quality.

Some things your mother told you about . . .

SERVICE

It's not the talented but the consecrated who serve God best!

One who earnestly serves God soon learns his own weakness.

Life is like a game of tennis—the player who serves well seldom loses.

The unpaid service you render humanity is exalting only as long as you don't mention it.

If we think we are too busy to serve God, remember— some day we will have to have time to die.

Serving the Lord is an investment that pays eternal dividends.

Little things done for God become great things.

Fill a place—not just a space.

Being a servant is something you choose.

Talent is God's gift to man—the use of talent is man's gift to God.

If you want good service, serve yourself.

Efficiency is the ability to avoid extra work by doing it right the first time.

Don't just live and let live, but live and help live.

A professional does his best, even when he doesn't feel like it.

They know him best who serve him best.

What you're doing is not work unless you'd rather be doing something else.

Service can never become slavery to one who loves.

Love is the doorway through which people pass from selfishness to service.

There are many who are willing to do great things for God, but few are willing to do little things.

If you want to succeed, make yourself useful.

You do not have to be perfect to work for the one who is.

It is a great pleasure to do good in secret and have it found out by accident.

Do not wait for extraordinary circumstances to do good; try to use ordinary situations.

We're not called to work for God but to let God work through us.

Service is love in action.

You cannot enjoy the harvest without first laboring in the field.

A busy man may not be happier than an idle one—he just does not have time to notice it.

There would be fewer empty hearts if there were more occupied minds and busier bodies.

It is not a tragedy to have just one talent—the tragedy is not using it.

A ship is safe in the harbor, but that is not the reason ships were built.

Those who walk with God won't run from people's needs.

Friendship is not for enjoyment only but also an opportunity for service.

Daily work takes on eternal value when it is done for God.

God didn't save you to sit but to serve.

Things insignificant to men may be great in the sight of God.

Some things your mother told you about . . .

SHARING

The measure of our love is the measure of our sacrifice.

Life takes on new meaning when we invest it in others.

We are not put on this earth to see through one another but to see one another through.

Every day we live is another opportunity to help someone else.

A sorrow shared is divided—a joy shared is doubled.

Whatever we share with another, regardless how little, enriches two persons.

When we forget about ourselves, we do things others will remember.

God can move mountains, but he needs our hands to do the work.

Those who care will share.

A recipe that is not shared will soon be forgotten—when shared it will be enjoyed for generations.

Other people enjoy sharing their skills with us—don't be too proud or ashamed to ask for help.

Blessed is the man who digs a well from which another may draw faith.

When you help out a man in trouble, you can be sure of one thing—he won't forget you the next time he's in trouble.

When your cup overflows, share it—don't waste it.

Putting your heart into other people's problems is better than putting your nose into their business.

A candle loses none of its light by lighting another candle.

The greatest privilege of strength is not ruling over others but protecting them.

Greatness lies not in trying to be somebody but in trying to help somebody.

The smallest dewdrop hanging from a grass blade is big enough to reflect the sunshine and the blue sky.

When you bring sunshine to others, you enjoy it yourself.

Compromise is the art of cutting a cake so that everyone believes they have gotten the biggest piece.

It's not what you have but what you do with it.

There's no greater loan than a sympathetic ear.

Every gift, though it be small, is in reality great if given with affection.

Generosity is giving more than you can; pride is taking less than you need.

Hold those you love with open hands.

When a person is down, an ounce of help is better than a pound of preaching.

Only love can be divided endlessly and still not be diminished.

Refusing to ask for help when you need it is refusing someone the chance to be helpful.

Sharing should be a twin to joy.

Not what we gain, but what we give, measures the worth of the life we live.

The lad who gave his loaves and fish did not go hungry.

No one can help everyone, but everyone can help someone.

If you give comfort to others, you'll know how to heal your own hurts.

If you have nothing to give, you can give encouragement.

Some things your mother told you about . . .

SIN

Those who would not fall into sin should never sit near the door of temptation.

To love a small sin is a great sin.

A man of courage is not ashamed to admit his faults, failures, and sins.

It is better to suffer wrong than to do it.

Little sins do mischief in a life.

Sin may start out as fun, but in the end it becomes a master.

Master that sin in your life or it will master you.

Don't trifle with sin—sin is no trifle.

Never plant a seed you are unwilling to reap.

Sin has the habit of running past the red signal before it stops.

Sinful pleasure can be like a hornet—ending with a sting.

You can't live out of the garbage can of sin and have a healthy soul.

A loose-living person keeps their diary in a loose-leaf binder.

A sorry sinner without repentance is still a sinner.

Sin never stands still—it always continues to grow.

People cannot sin without causing the innocent to suffer.

Sin causes the cup of joy to spring a leak.

What starts out as innocent fun often ends up as big trouble.

Forbidden fruit may taste sweeter, but it gets rotten a whole lot sooner.

To bear good fruit, clear out the weeds of sin.

The devil always paints sin in many attractive colors.

Delilah didn't want Samson's hair; she wanted his scalp.

Confession of sin is not a weakness but a sign of strength.

Forbidden fruit creates many jams.

If you flee from sin, you won't fall into it.

Some things your mother told you about . . .
SMILING

No one is beyond the ministry of a kindly smile.

Smiles are more becoming than frowns.

Put on a smile—one size fits all.

Smiles are magnetic—they draw people together.

A smile is the whisper of a laugh.

A smile is the lighting system of the face and the heating system of the heart.

If there is a smile in your heart, your face will show it.

Of all the things you wear, your smile is the most important.

A man who doesn't like to smile at strangers shouldn't run a store.

The best kind of wrinkles indicate where smiles have been.

Smile now—you may not feel like it later.

Smiles never go up in price nor down in value.

There is always something all people can give to others— a smile.

All people smile in the same language.

A smile doesn't cost a cent, but it gains a lot of interest.

A warm smile and wholesome laughter have great face value.

The best way to ease tension between two people is to smile.

A smile is worth a thousand words.

Smile awhile and give your frown a rest.

A person who smiles when everything goes wrong has probably thought of someone to blame it on.

Some things your mother told you about . . .
SPEAKING IN PUBLIC

We all love the speaker who says, "To make a long story short, . . ." and then does.

If you can't state the problem in a few sentences, chances are you don't know what the problem is.

You don't have to listen long to realize some speeches have nothing to say.

Love simple speech as much as you hate shallow thinking.

Don't use a gallon of water to express a spoonful of thought.

Some things your mother told you about . . .
SPORTS

The best coaches are always in the stands.

It's impossible to play tennis without raising a racket.

The side that wins is not always the best side.

If you can't win the race, make the one ahead of you break the record.

For some, golf is just a method of beating around the bush.

Some things your mother told you about . . .
STABILITY

Flowers that bend toward the sun do so even on cloudy days.

When you jump for joy, beware no one moves the ground beneath you.

Those rooted in Christ will not be uprooted by the world.

The Lord calls us to stand, though not always to understand.

You lose your stability when you leave the Rock of Ages.

To bear the Spirit's fruit, don't let sin take root.

Some things your mother told you about . . .

STUBBORNNESS

An unfailing mark of a blockhead is the chip on his shoulder.

To walk in our own way is to run away from God.

A stiff neck usually supports an empty head.

The only thing worse than a stubborn man who is wrong is a stubborn man who is right.

When a mule has it, no one calls it willpower.

The best way to win an argument is to start out by being right.

Jonah gave God a headache and the whale a stomachache.

Some things your mother told you about . . .

SUCCESS

The wheels of progress are seldom turned by cranks.

Success is sweet, but it requires a lot of sweat.

Most people are in favor of progress—it's change they can't stand.

The roughest road oftentimes goes straight to the top of the hill.

The road to success is paved with good intentions that were carried out.

Success is built on the ability to do better than good enough.

Popularity results from pleasing people, but greatness comes from pleasing God.

The great man is he who does not lose his childlike heart.

If yesterday seems great to you, you haven't done much today.

Great men have convictions—ordinary men have only opinions.

Success comes to those who decide to do a thing—and then do it.

Success is determined by determination.

To succeed, work your tongue little, your hands much, and your brain most.

It is not success that God rewards but faithfulness in doing his will.

Prosperity has a strong tendency to draw the heart away from God.

It's a great feeling to stand on top of the hill, even if the wind does blow off your hat.

Success not only gives one a big head—it gives some a big stomach.

There are many paths to the top of the mountain, but the view is always the same.

Progress has little to do with speed but much with direction.

Success lies not in achieving what you aim at but in aiming at what you ought to achieve.

A man can't make a place for himself in the sun if he keeps taking refuge under the family tree.

The man of the hour spent many days and nights getting there.

You are not obligated to succeed—you are obligated only to do your best.

True winners are those who have learned how to lose.

Success consists of getting up just one more time than you fall.

Look forward to some success, not backward at any failure.

You lose a lot of battles in the process of winning the war.

Achievers are not born—they are made.

The most successful person is the one who wins over an enemy without striking a blow.

Success and achievement are impossible unless you have control over yourself.

All professionals were at one time amateurs.

High expectation is one of the first steps to success.

If your goal is to get on top of the world, you're aiming too low.

When you get to the top, remember who helped you get there.

When the load feels heavy, it's a sign you're climbing.

Though no one can go back and make a brand-new start, anyone can start from now and make a brand-new end.

Success may be under the next layer of stone. Even if it isn't, the digging is fine exercise.

The first step to success is accepting responsibility.

The laurels of today's struggles make sure shrouds for anyone who sleeps in them.

The man on top of the mountain doesn't fall there.

Work harder at being what you should be than at hiding what you are.

Spiritual triumphs are not won by people in easy chairs.

Every great achievement was once impossible.

Nothing is achieved before it is thoroughly attempted.

The reward of a thing well done is to have done it.

Measure success not by the things you have, but by the things you have for which you would not take money.

Success comes to those who are neither afraid to fail nor discouraged by failures.

One of the biggest troubles with success is that its recipe is often the same as that for a nervous breakdown.

When you do what God tells you to do, you are a success.

Don't be discouraged by failure or satisfied with success.

progress on... i... stick it's neck out...

A small **HINT** is worth a **TON** of Advice

It is bad Manners to talk when your Mouth is full and your Head is **EMPTY**

T

Some things your mother told you about . . .
TACT

Blunt words often have sharp edges.

It takes a great man to give sound advice tactfully, but a greater one to accept it gracefully.

Be wiser than other people, if you can, but do not tell them that you are.

Some things your mother told you about . . .
TEACHING

It takes a lot to teach a little.

The best teacher follows his own instructions.

Those who teach must be teachable.

If you don't live it—don't teach it.

You can lead a horse to water, but you cannot make him think.

A good teacher is better than many books.

A good teacher's teaching is like throwing a stone into the water—the ripples never seem to cease.

A teacher is a person who can take many live wires and see that they are well grounded.

Some things your mother told you about . . .

TEENAGERS

The main trouble with youth is that it's practically over by the time you realize you've got it.

People who keep saying "nothing is impossible" don't have teenagers.

If you want to recapture your youth, cut off his allowance.

Some things your mother told you about . . .

TEMPER

Temper makes a person speak his mind when he should be minding his speech.

Every time you lose your temper, you advertise yourself.

A quarrel is quickly settled when deserted by one party.

No matter how bad the situation, you can lose your temper and make it worse.

Some things your mother told you about . . .

TEMPERANCE

Be watchful over yourself when you are alone.

When alone, watch your thoughts; when with your family, watch your temper; when in company, watch your tongue.

Being brave never goes out of style.

Some things your mother told you about . . .

TEMPTATION

Obstacles are what you see when you take your eyes off the goal.

Forbidden fruit makes for a bad jam.

When you flee temptation, do not leave a forwarding address.

No matter how strong you think you are, avoid temptation.

Never put the welcome mat out for an evil thought.

Resisting temptation is more than just putting it off until nobody is looking.

It's easier to stay away from temptation than to withstand temptation.

To withstand temptation, stand with God.

Lust always brags about the pleasure and forgets to mention the pain.

No virtue is ever so strong that it is beyond temptation.

Opportunity knocks often, but temptation walks right in.

Temptation, unlike opportunities, will give second and third chances.

Linger at the well of temptation and you'll find yourself drinking of evil and sin.

Opportunity knocks once—temptation leans on the doorbell.

Some things your mother told you about . . .

THANKS

Thanks is worthless when it gushes like oil.

A compliment is verbal sunshine.

Never let the abundance of God's gifts cause you to forget the giver.

Don't throw a stone into a well from which you have drunk.

A grateful heart will be a happy heart.

He who is not thankful for little is not worthy of much.

Thankfulness is the soil in which joy thrives.

If you can't think of anything to be thankful for, you have a poor memory.

When you think of all that's good, give thanks to God.

Thankfulness is a sure guarantee of a serene soul.

Be thankful if your job is a little harder than you like. A razor cannot be sharpened on a piece of velvet.

Happiness comes when we stop wailing about the troubles we have and offer thanks for all the troubles we do not have.

We should be thankful not only for good things but also for the things we think are bad as well.

Those blessings are the sweetest that are won with prayers and worn with thanks.

There are two times to thank the Lord—when you feel like it and when you don't.

The secret of happiness is to count your blessings, not your birthdays.

Take everything with gratitude but nothing for granted.

He enjoys much who is thankful for much.

To deserve thanks and not get it is better than to get it and not deserve it.

Some people, instead of being thankful when their cup runs over, pray for a bigger cup.

Instead of complaining about the thorns on roses, be thankful for the roses among the thorns.

Don't blame God for having created the tiger, but thank him for not having given it wings.

Some things your mother told you about . . .
THINKING

If you clutter up your mind with little things, will there be any room left for the big things?

The happiness of your life depends upon the quality of your thoughts.

A minute of thought is worth more than an hour of talk.

A mind unemployed is a mind unenjoyed.

It's good to have an open mind if you know what to let in.

The mind is like a window shade—the more you open it, the more light you let in.

The person who often loses his head doesn't miss it.

It's human to have your mind wander, but the trouble comes when you follow it.

You cannot escape the results of your own thoughts.

The ancestry of every action is thought.

An open mind is not the same as an empty mind.

You should have an open mind, but not open at both ends.

A grateful mind is a great mind.

Healthiness of mind is essential to holiness of life.

A right attitude toward God fosters the right attitudes toward your family and others.

Think seldom of your enemies, often of your friends, and constantly of Christ.

Be careful of your thoughts; they may become words at any moment.

We cannot think crooked and live straight.

The person who thinks he can fool everybody has a short career ahead of him.

The face is the index to the mind.

Guilt is always suspicious.

Memory is the sheath in which the sword of the Lord is kept.

Memory alone is a poor substitute for thought.

It takes a strong mind to hold an unruly tongue.

Forethought spares afterthought.

An open mind is fine—if it isn't accompanied by an open mouth.

A narrow-minded man doesn't hold opinions—opinions hold him.

The soul is dyed the color of our leisure thoughts.

To have a healthy mind, base your thinking on the Word of God and the guidance of the Holy Spirit.

Empty pockets never held anyone back; it is only empty heads and hearts that do it.

The faster you think, the slower you should speak.

Give every man thy ear, but never thy voice.

Don't dismiss a good idea simply because you don't like the source.

Don't allow your mouth to say something your head doesn't understand.

Take time to think where you're going, or you may not like where you end up.

Successful folks don't just entertain thoughts; they put them to work.

What comes out of your mouth depends on what goes into your mind.

There are two kinds of people who don't say much—those who are quiet and those who talk a lot.

Find an idea big enough to live for and you will never be unemployed.

Evil thoughts are not sinful until you harbor them.

Right thinking leads to right living.

Keep out of your life whatever keeps Christ out of your mind.

Some things your mother told you about . . .

TIME

We always have enough time if we use it right.

Time and money are alike—both need to be spent wisely.

A pound of gold can never buy a second of time.

You can take a day off, but you can never put it back.

The moment may be temporary, but the memory is forever.

Time spent in mere regret is worse than wasted.

A stitch in time saves a lot of embarrassment.

Counting time is not so important as making time count.

Sometimes it takes more time to remodel than to build from scratch.

Lost time is never found again.

What makes some people tick can turn into a time bomb.

God always speaks to those who have time to listen.

A person who is a slave to the clock will never be a master of time.

Time misspent is not lived but lost.

Yesterday is gone; tomorrow is a gamble; today is a sure thing—make the most of it.

The texture of eternity is woven on the looms of time.

Preserve the past—reveal the present—create the future.

God wants our precious time—not our spare time.

Most of our troubles come from too much time on our hands and not enough on our knees.

Time may be a healer, but it's no beauty specialist.

The worst thing about history is that every time it repeats itself, the prices go up.

Time is the only thing we all possess equally.

You always have time for things you put first.

The best way to pay for a lovely moment is to enjoy it.

Sunrises are just as pretty as sunsets, but they aren't timed right for most people to see them.

Seek time for the things that outlast it.

You should take time before time takes you.

One today is worth a dozen tomorrows.

The man who makes the best use of his time has more time to spare.

Time is like a snowflake—it disappears while we are trying to decide what to do with it.

No time is ever wasted that makes two people better friends.

Some things your mother told you about . . .

TONGUE

Better to slip with the foot than with the tongue.

The person who thinks before they speak is silent most of the time.

Speech is silver—silence is golden.

If your foot slips, you can recover your balance—if your tongue slips, you cannot recall your words.

It takes a wise person to know what not to say—and then not to say it.

One way to store up knowledge is to keep your mouth shut.

If you have nothing good to say, don't speak at all.

Silence leaves no sad memories.

Observe keenly, think constantly, talk less, and say more.

The art of eloquence is to know when to keep still.

A sharp tongue can be a deadly weapon.

Confine your tongue lest it confine you.

A still tongue makes a wise head.

By putting your best foot forward, you keep it out of your mouth.

Profanity is the mark of a conversational cripple.

It's better to bite your tongue than to have a biting tongue.

A fool always has an answer on the tip of his tongue.

A fool's tongue is always long enough to cut his throat.

If you have something nice to say, anytime is the right time to say it.

Some things your mother told you about . . .

TRIALS

Meeting God in our trials is better than getting out of them.

The diamond cannot be polished without friction nor the man perfected without trials.

Difficulties show what men are.

The more difficult a situation, the greater your opportunity to learn and develop.

Happiness is not the absence of conflict but the ability to cope with it.

The thickest clouds bring the heaviest showers of blessing.

When troubles call you, call God.

The soul would have no rainbow if the eyes had no tears.

We need a few clouds in our lives to make beautiful sunsets.

Sorrows are often our best teachers.

Trials are the soil in which faith grows.

Trials test trust.

Spiritual power comes through pressure.

God is more concerned about your response to a problem than he is about removing the problem.

Experienced sailors are able to sail in all types of weather.

When suffering pain, remember—the pearl starts as a pain in the oyster's stomach.

The same hammer that shatters glass also forges steel.

It takes both rain and sunshine to make a rainbow.

To realize the worth of the anchor, we need to feel the storm.

There are no shortcuts to any place worth going to.

Only when we walk in the dark can we see the stars.

The roots grow deep when the wind blows strong.

Most of the shadows of life are caused by standing in our own sunshine.

Rough paths often lead to desirable destinations.

Almost every path has a puddle.

When it gets dark enough, the stars always come out.

Don't think you are on the right road just because it's a well-beaten path.

God would have no furnace if there was no gold to refine.

With extraordinary trials come extraordinary grace.

The wounded oyster mends his shell with a pearl.

Trials don't seem to come one by one—rather all at once.

Anyone can be at the helm when the sea is calm.

When a shower brings a rainbow, we hardly remember getting wet.

The bend in the road is not the end of the road unless you fail to make the turn.

A clay pot in the sun will always be a clay pot—when going through the white heat of the furnace, it becomes porcelain.

In every desert of trial, God has an oasis of comfort.

Some things your mother told you about . . .

TROUBLE

Never trouble trouble until trouble troubles you.

Circumstances do not make a man; they reveal what he's made of.

Remember the tea kettle—up to her neck in hot water, yet she can still sing.

Troubles that you borrow soon become your own.

You can't keep trouble from coming, but you don't have to give it a chair to sit on.

Troubles depend on your part of the view—a bunion looks good to the foot doctor.

Be too large for worry, too noble for anger, too strong for fear, and too happy to permit the presence of trouble.

Nothing lasts forever—not even your troubles.

The more a diamond is cut, the more it sparkles.

Thorns don't prick you unless you lean against them.

Spend more time on the solution than you do on the problem.

Obstacles seem large when you take your eyes off the Lord.

Great triumphs are born out of great troubles.

Trouble is like muddy water—be patient, don't stir it, and it will soon clear up.

There is no strength where there is no struggle.

Troubles are opportunities for progress.

Never meet trouble halfway—it's quite capable of making the entire journey alone.

Some things your mother told you about . . .

TRUST

Trust everything to him who can never be taken from you and who will never leave you.

Even better than to understand God is to trust him.

Let your testing time be a trusting time.

Trust in God's power prevents panic.

If others do not trust you, you have lost almost everything.

You can't steal second base if you don't take your foot off first.

The closer you live to God, the more you will trust him.

Some things your mother told you about . . .

TRUTH

The devil has many tools, and a lie is a handle that fits them all.

Opinions are a dime a dozen, but truth is priceless.

Even a broken watch is right twice a day.

When you shoot an arrow of truth, dip its point in honey.

Truth is more precious than time.

He who approves a white lie will find the shade growing darker.

Truth has to change hands only a few times to become fiction.

To know Christ is to know the truth.

Strive for peace if possible, but truth at any cost.

Sincerity is no substitute for truth.

When truth is in your way, you are on the wrong way.

It is better to declare the truth and be rejected than to withhold it just to be accepted.

A bald truth is a whole lie.

Stretching the truth won't make it last longer.

When truth is mixed with tenderness, it's easier to take.

Truth and oil always come to the top.

Often silence does more harm to truth than do lies.

A bird cannot FLY if it is in the egg

...n Pain Medic... ...ive as a mothe... KISS

People who JUMP often land on a lie

Some things your mother told you about . . .

UNDERSTANDING

Never take down a fence until you know the reason it was put up.

It is better to understand little than misunderstand a lot.

When you listen to both sides, there is always hope.

If you do not know where you are going, you will not know if and when you get there.

Everything has its beauty but not everyone sees it.

You cannot tell the depth of the well by the length of the handle on the pump.

The biggest step you can take is when you meet others halfway.

Get your directions before you try for the distance.

Understanding is a two-way street.

To understand how a person ticks, you must understand what winds him up.

A true vision is what you see not only with your eyes but also with your heart.

When things come with strings attached, be sure you tie up the loose ends.

Some things your mother told you about . . .

UNSTABLE PEOPLE

Trying to do everything at once makes everything go wrong at once.

A person who agrees with everything you say needs to be watched.

A man who is on a wild goose chase all his life never feathers much of a nest.

A small HINT is worth a TON of Advice

It is bad Manners to talk when your Mouth is full and your Head is EMPTY

Some things your mother told you about . . .

VICTORY

For every cloud in life, God gives a rainbow.

Victories are not won by going downhill—unless you are a skier.

Some things your mother told you about . . .
WISDOM

What a fool does in the end, the wise man does in the beginning.

Horse sense keeps you from betting on a man.

The honey of wisdom is often gathered from the thorns of adversity.

One pound of learning requires ten pounds of common sense to apply it.

If you don't use your head, you'll use your heels a lot.

Fads come and go—common sense goes on forever.

God gave us a Bible and a brain—he expects us to use them both.

Do not insult the mother alligator until after you have crossed the river.

There is no substitute for good old common sense.

It is possible to make a sound argument without making a lot of noise.

Wisdom is knowing what to do next—virtue is doing it.

More important than having authority is knowing how to use it.

Trust in God, but lock your car.

A willing heart must be controlled by a wise head.

A person with horse sense does not trot with the crowd.

Wisdom often comes disguised as silence.

No matter how good your bait, you can't get a bite unless you fish where the fish are.

If you are filled with pride, you'll have no room for wisdom.

Some things your mother told you about . . .

WITNESSING

Christ never told his disciples to stay at home and wait for sinners to come to them.

Be simply a reflector of Christ, not a radiator.

The best witnessing is done not by our words but by our walk.

Lighthouses don't ring bells to get attention—they just shine.

If Christ is worth having, he's worth sharing.

Shine like a glowworm if you can't be a star.

Some things your mother told you about . . .
WORDS

An echo may be accurate, but it doesn't tell you anything.

The size of your foot has very little to do with your ability to get it into your mouth.

Silent gratitude is not much use to anyone.

There is nothing wrong with having nothing to say unless you say it aloud.

The use of profanity is unreasonable and unchristian, offending both God and man.

A foul mouth is the mark of a polluted soul.

A good word is as easily said as a bad one.

The less you talk, the more you are listened to.

Swallowing angry words is a lot easier than having to eat them.

Words are like water—easy to pour, impossible to recover.

Language, like linen, looks best when it is clean.

What is in the well of your heart will show up in the bucket of your speech.

No one can jump down your throat if you keep your mouth shut.

The most effective answer to an insult is silence.

Words are like a prescription dosage—more is not necessarily better.

A wise person soon learns that silence can't be misquoted.

There's a big difference between free speech and cheap talk.

A well-chosen word can speak volumes.

Kind words are the music of the world.

Daggers draw blood, but sharp words wound the heart.

Remember, if you can't write it down and sign it, don't say it.

Kind words are short to speak, but their echoes are endless.

All good words and intentions are of little value unless put into practice.

Words spoken in love need no interpreter.

Words are the hummingbirds of imagination.

Language may be a vehicle of thought, but in some cases it's just an empty wagon.

Kind words and kind deeds keep life's garden free of weeds.

Live so that you would not be ashamed to sell the family parrot to the town gossip.

Like fire, words can either burn or warm.

The less you say, the more people will remember.

The greatest impression is often made by silence.

Some of the best arguments are spoiled by people who know what they are talking about.

Speak well of people and you'll never need to whisper.

You can speak to the point without being sharp.

A sheep that does much bleating loses many mouthfuls of food.

An empty barrel makes the loudest noise.

Good words cost nothing but are worth much.

Trying to get a word in edgewise when some are talking is like trying to thread a needle with the sewing machine running.

Gentle words fall lightly but have great weight.

The fly that buzzes the loudest usually gets swatted.

The better you know what you're talking about, the more simply you can put it.

Talk slowly but aim quickly.

Some things your mother told you about . . .

WORK

If you don't scale the mountain, you can't see the view.

Shells can be found on the beach, but for pearls you must dive.

Often the thrill of life comes from the difficult work well done.

It's not enough to light a fire—you must put fuel on it.

Take your work seriously but yourself lightly.

Don't let work divorce itself from imagination.

Greener pastures often have higher fences.

Dewdrops do God's work as much as the thunderstorms.

There are two ways to get to the top of an oak tree—climb it, or sit on an acorn and wait.

God gives the ingredients for our daily bread, but he expects us to do the baking.

No one ever climbed a hill by looking at it.

The woodpecker is a success because he uses his head and keeps working until he finishes his job.

A good anvil is not afraid of the hammer.

Nothing comes out of a bag that you do not put into it.

Hard work is nothing more than an accumulation of easy things you didn't do when you should have.

The world's work is not done by giants but by men who fetch and carry.

The Lord blesses efforts, not wishes.

He who chops wood warms himself twice.

No horse gets anywhere until it is harnessed.

Do more than you are paid for before expecting to be paid for more than you do.

The world owes us nothing—it was here first.

He who rolls up his sleeves seldom loses his shirt.

The world is blessed by those who do things—not by those who merely talk about it.

You may not always be able to do something brilliant, but you can do something that is useful.

Variety is the spice of life, but monotony provides the groceries.

You are never lonely at the bottom of the ladder.

Just because a man is working hard doesn't mean he is accomplishing a lot.

The virtues of work are extolled most loudly by those without blisters.

A person shows what he is by what he does with what he has.

It isn't enough to say the river is dirty—what are you doing to clean it?

It is a rough road that leads to the heights of greatness.

The way to get anywhere is to start where you are.

Every job is a self-portrait of the person who did it. Autograph your work with excellence.

If the wind doesn't blow—row.

Both tears and sweat are salty, but they render different results—tears will get sympathy, sweat will get you a change.

Fortune may find a pot, but only work can make it boil.

Never seek a larger and better crop—seek better seeds.

He who burns the candle at both ends is not very bright.

Too many people make the mistake of hitting the hay when they should be out making it.

Never pray for more than you are willing to work for.

Take a lesson from the clock—it passes time by keeping its hands busy.

Pray for what you want, but work for what you need.

You can go anywhere if you build the road.

When a man works like a horse, everyone rides him.

Diligence is the mother of good luck.

When love and skill work together, expect a miracle.

We cannot create the wind or set it in motion, but we can set our sails to catch it when it comes.

No one ever drowned in sweat.

Some things your mother told you about . . .

WORRY

Worry ends where faith begins.

Worry empties a day of its strength—not of its trouble.

To worry about what we can't help or change is useless.

Worry requires as much or more energy than work does.

If it's worth worrying about, it's worth praying about.

Anxiety does not empty tomorrow of its trials—it simply empties today of its joy.

Worry is the interest paid on trouble before it becomes due.

Worry is self-centered. Those who worry the least are those who do the most for other people.

Worry pulls tomorrow's cloud over today's sunshine.

Most of our worries are reruns.

A bow bent too much is easily broken.

Worry is like carrying a load of feathers we think are lead.

Worry is today's mouse eating tomorrow's cheese.

Worry only heats the bearings—it does not generate the steam.

Some things your mother told you about . . .

WRONG

Thinking upon wrong is the source of many evil deeds.

We commit two wrongs when we fail to right a wrong.

It's better to be approximately right than precisely wrong.

You cannot do wrong and be truly happy.

Any wrong we do toward others is done toward God.

You can't do wrong and feel right.

To err is human, but to really screw up you need a computer.

When we do wrong, we suffer, but we also cause others to suffer.

Our wrongdoings are not due to circumstances but to our weakness.

A bird cannot FLY if it is in the egg

in Pain Medic ... re as a mother KISS

People who JUMP ... often land on a ...

Some things your mother told you about . . .

YOUTH

There's nothing wrong with the younger generation that twenty years will not cure.

All the wild oats sowed as a youth will have to be reaped sooner or later.

A drizzle is two drips going steady.

An icicle is a drip that got caught in a draft.

A young branch takes on all the bends that one gives it.

Prisons are a monument to neglected youth.

Juvenile delinquents are other people's children.

Youth prefers to learn the hard way, and some people never seem to grow old.

Adolescence is that period when children feel their parents should be told the facts of life.

The truly thoughtful teenager leaves enough gas in the car so you can make it to the gas station.

It's often hard to get the rising generation up in the morning.

No one has more of a driving ambition than a teenager wanting his own car.

You are young and useful at any age if you are still planning for tomorrow.

If you want to stay youthful—stay useful.

To avoid the mistakes of youth, draw from the wisdom of age.

You're only young once; after that, you have to make up some other excuse for your actions.

In youth we learn; in age we understand.

You are only young once, but once is enough if you work it right.

When teaching young people, you're not just spending time—you're investing it.

Youth is when you are always hunting for greener pastures, and middle age is when you can barely mow the one you've got.

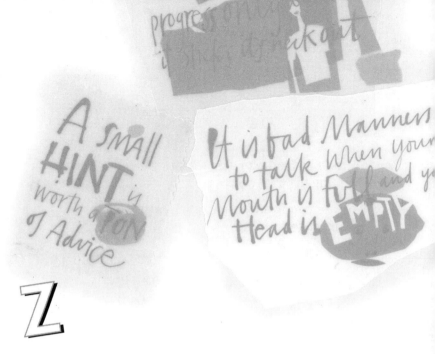

progress only ... [it sticks its neck out]

A small HINT is worth a TON of Advice

It is bad Manners to talk when your Mouth is full and your Head is EMPTY

Z

Some things your mother told you about . . .

ZEAL

Zeal that is spiritual is also charitable.

Our zeal should never be greater than our wisdom.

Zeal without knowledge is the sister of folly.